THE CREATION
OF MUSIC

The
CREATION of
MUSIC

BRITIAN BELL

This is a work of fiction. All of the characters,
organizations, and events portrayed in this novel
are either products of the author's imagination or
are used fictitiously.

Britianbell.com

Cover and interior designed by Edgel Barrientos.

Names: Bell, Britian, author.
Title: The Creation of Music / Britian Bell.
Description: First edition 2024.
Identifiers: ISBN 979-8-218-42365-0 (paperback) |
ISBN 979-8-218-42615-6 (hardcover)

This novel is dedicated to Bartolomeo Cristofori (1655-1731), the man who invented the piano. The true story of his life was never recorded and has not been passed down through history. All that is known about him is his work as a hired hand at the Florentine Court in Florence, Italy, and his invention of the piano almost entirely on his own.

Today's piano is largely the same as the instrument Bartolomeo built. And has only grown in dominance as the king of all instruments. One man's work changed music forever.

My hope with this story is to shed light on what Bartolomeo Cristofori accomplished in his life and the determination and support required for him to do so. I want this novel to honor his legacy and give him the gratitude of everyone touched by music at some point in their lives.

Thank you.

To enrich your reading experience, be sure to listen to
The Soundtrack for The Creation of Music.

You can stream the album anywhere you currently listen
to music: Apple Music, Spotify, Youtube.com, Pandora,
Amazon Music, Tidal, Deezer, and more!

CHAPTER
One

1664

*B*artolomeo Cristofori sits among the rows of young students waiting to be called on to introduce themselves. Sunlight peeks through the linen curtains. An air of excitement pervades the classroom. Another year of school offers boundless opportunities to create new friendships and blow the dust off old ones, and Bart is eager to get started. The teacher stands in front of her desk. She seems welcoming. He likes her smile.

"Adele," Ms. Ricci calls out. When her name is called, Adele, a shy and petite nine-year-old girl with blinding blond hair and big eyes, stands from her desk and beams. Her homemade dress brushes the legs of each student she passes by on her way to the front of the room. "Hi, Adele. Tell us your full name."

"My name is Adele Bianchi," she says in a sweet voice.

"What a beautiful name you have! What do you do for fun?"

"Um," Adele bites her bottom lip as she watches her feet dig into the classroom floor, "I like to play with my friends."

"Oh, and what do you play?"

"Hide and seek!" she says with more confidence.

"That sounds fun, Adele! Thank you for sharing with us. You may return to your seat now." Adele darts quickly back to her chair in the middle of the room, her golden pigtails flying in the breeze she leaves in her wake.

"Bartolomeo," Ms. Ricci calls out now.

Yes! He confidently stands from his chair—purposely chosen in the front of the room.

"Tell us—"

"My name is Bart Cristofori, and I'm an inventor!" Speaking with bold enthusiasm, Bart cuts off Ms. Ricci. He is probably the most excited kid in Padua, Italy, to be in school again.

"Really? What do you invent, Bart?" Ms. Ricci asks.

Within the time it takes to blink he unfolds his leather bag and quickly starts digging with both hands for an item that holds a special place in his heart. "This!" he says. His round and bright face exuding excitement.

"Are those glasses?"

"Not just any glasses. These can change colors," he explains.

"Oh really?" she says doubtfully.

"Want to try them on?" He offers them to her.

"Sure," she says, unable to turn down such an intriguing offer.

He hands his precious invention to his new teacher with care. She gently holds them in her hands, mimicking Bart's care, and places them over her eyes. He explains to her to look directly forward. "Ready?"

"Yes."

"Look down," he instructs.

She does as he says and immediately covers her mouth and gasps.

"What do you see?" Bart's heart pounds in anticipation.

"Everything is blue!" she says with both wonder and surprise.

His face gleams with pride that he has managed to impress his teacher. He detects a note of awe in the silence that has fallen over the classroom. Glancing quickly out at the faces of his fellow students, it thrills him to see that each one seems fully engrossed in Ms. Ricci's experience with the glasses he invented.

He looks back at Ms. Ricci. "Now look up only a little bit," he directs.

Ms. Ricci lifts her head ever so slightly. "Wow." She smiles. "Now everything is red."

"Cool, isn't it?" Bart asks. Rather than answer, to his dismay she tilts her head back as far as she can. "No!" he shouts. "Don't do that!"

Silence befalls the small classroom, and an awkward tension fills the air between Ms. Ricci and Bart.

"I'm so sorry, Bart," she says, jerking her head down and taking the glasses off. "I didn't realize." She hands them back to Bart.

Fighting tears, he says, "It's okay." Folding the glasses, he stuffs them back into his bag. Then slowly, with a downcast posture, he walks back to his seat feeling exposed. *Why did she do that?*

Bart is barely aware as Ms. Ricci introduces the rest of the students in her small classroom. The morning passes, and at lunchtime the ten of them line up, ready to leave the room. But as the others file out in pursuit of the cafeteria, Ms. Ricci catches Bart's eye and mouths, "Wait."

He is reseated at his desk when she gently approaches him.

"Bart, I am so sorry for looking past where you told me. I was excited by your invention," she says with a proud smile.

Moved by her gentleness and compliment, he meets her eyes. "That's okay, Ms. Ricci."

"It isn't any of my business, so you don't have to tell me if you don't want to, but you know what I saw—the—the—"

"Drawing," Bart supplies the word Ms. Ricci was looking for.

"Yes, of a girl. Who is she?"

"My mama." Bart lowers his gaze, feeling his heart squeeze and his throat tighten. He fights an urge to flee.

Ms. Ricci places her hand on her chest. "You must love your mother so much. I can only imagine how much she loves you, too," she says with a vibrant tone. Bart doesn't return her smile, but looks at his desk now, waiting for her to dismiss him.

"Loved," he clarifies. His pulse beats like a stampede of cattle. He knew this would come up but hoped it wouldn't on the first day. He has never liked it when adults talk to him about his mother. He doesn't know what to say, and his emotions never seem to meet their expectations.

"What do you mean?" she asks.

"She died. Can I go?"

"Oh, oh, I'm so sorry," she gasps. "Yes, yes, of course you may go. I'm so sorry for keeping you." Stepping away, she gives him room to leave his desk, and he wastes no time, bolting from the classroom in search of his friends and food.

"How did you do that?" Bart's best friend, Marco, asks as they hold their trays for the two lunch ladies to serve the food.

"Do what?" Bart asks with feigned innocence.

"You know... invent those special glasses."

"Oh. I used some old pieces of stained glass from the church that I found broken on the sidewalk," he says as they find a seat at a table by themselves.

Padua is a thriving city despite the countrywide economic crisis. Padua also prioritizes education, so the school is sufficiently funded by the church for fall and spring sessions. Bart knows this from listening to adults talk. Along with Marco, he also knows to eat all he can at school since money and food are still scarce at home. Both boys had lost a fair amount of weight over the summer, sharpening the edge of their appetites.

"That is crazy, Bart. You are so smart!" Marco raves, his wide mouth partially agape.

"Thanks, but I'm not really."

"What was wrong when Ms. Ricci looked all the way up?" Marco presses.

Not this again. "Nothing." Bart looks away, avoiding Marco's curious gaze. "I don't want to talk about it."

"Okay, no problem. I sure missed you the last couple of months." Easy natured, Marco changes the subject. "I had to work with Papa at the leather shop all summer." He cringes. "The smell of leather—" Breaking off, Marco fake gags. "It was horrible."

When Marco laughs, Bart joins in. "I didn't have to work in a leather shop, but my father said since I'm nine, I have to start doing all the chores around the house." Bart rolls his eyes. "It wasn't that bad, though."

Bart and his father have been the only two in the Cristofori household since his mother died two years ago. But, truthfully, he feels he's raising himself. His father leaves early in the morning every day and comes home late from work. Bart has a better relationship with his imagination than his own father. His father does pay the bills and provides a safe place to live, but that is all. Like Bart, he is consumed with grief, and although Bart is young, he can see how it stifles his and his father's ability to be of any emotional support for one another.

"Compared to leatherworking, doing chores sounds great. I would have traded with you," Marco says, and they both laugh.

♩♪ 🎹 ♪♪♫

The end of the day arrives speedily for Bart. He could be learning something all the time and never grow bored in the classroom. Math is especially interesting to him. Thankfully, the subject has become more of a priority for his age group, and as he walks down the steps, leaving the school behind him, he feels a burst of impatience for tomorrow.

"Bart!"

The shout comes behind him, and he turns immediately, seeing Adele rushing toward him, legs pumping, blond pigtails flying.

"Hi, Adele," he says, feeling his heartbeat quicken.

"Hi," she says breathlessly. "Wait, can you?" she gasps, then bends over with her hands on her knees in an effort to catch her breath. After about thirty seconds, she straightens and says, "Okay. I'm ready."

"What did you want?" Bart asks as they walk along the edge of the cobblestone street together. They don't know each other well, only a few words ever spoken between them.

"Nothing. I want to walk with you." Adele is beaming with pride as she walks along with Bart. Her bold and confident posture is almost like gravity pulling him closer to her. *She is so pretty.*

"Okay. Where do you live?"

"That way." She points her finger in the air in a circular motion.

"That's everywhere?"

"I don't know where my house is from here. My mama is picking me up from the park. That way." This time, she points confidently in front of them.

"Perfect. I live by the park," he says, more excitedly than intended.

"I've never seen you there before?"

"That is because I never go," he explains.

"Why?" she asks with a confused face.

"Because I like to build things."

"You don't like to play?"

"Yeah, but playing by yourself isn't fun."

"You have no brothers or sisters?"

Bart feels her curious gaze. She's pressing him, the way Ms. Ricci did, and it only validates his preference for being alone. "No." He answers Adele without looking at her. "I almost did, but they died the same time my mama did." The tragic accident that stole his mother and his little brother at birth. He can still remember the screams coming from his parents' room when the surgeon arrived to try and save the baby, but it was too late.

Red-faced, Adele apologizes. "I'm sorry, Bart. I didn't know. I don't have any either."

Adele is only the second kid in Bart's small class to know about the accident now, and Marco only knows because despite Bart's refusal to ever talk about it, a child can't keep that kind of secret from their best friend.

They arrive at the park none too soon, easing the awkwardness between them. Bart's home calls his name, but not as loudly as Adele. "Bart!" she shouts as she sprints toward the swings in the playground. "Aren't you going to play with me?"

He rolls his eyes but can't deny his urge to stay with her. Rushing to Adele's side, he sits in a swing and pushes off the ground.

Over the next half hour, they each try and swing higher than the other before finally jumping out of their seats and finding the nearest bench to catch their breath. "Having fun, aren't you?" Adele pokes Bart's shoulder with her own.

"Yes!" He returns the gesture.

"You are a really good inventor," she says admiringly.

"You think so?" He glances at her, flattered.

"For sure. Those glasses seemed so amazing. You made Ms. Ricci gasp," Adele says with awe drenching her tone.

To his relief she doesn't ask what Ms. Ricci saw. "I know." Bart laughs, chest expanding with pride. "Do you like to do anything besides play?" he asks, and then drops his gaze. *What a dumb question.*

Adele seems to consider for a moment, before answering, "I like to help my mama in our garden."

"You like to grow things?"

"Yes! But I also like bugs, especially butterflies. They are so precious!" Her voice rises in a delighted squeal, even as she wiggles with laughter.

Bart smiles at her cute infatuation with butterflies. *She is special.* The thought flashes across his brain, making him feel warm inside.

"Do you like to do anything besides build things?" She looks expectantly at him.

"I like looking at instruments, musical instruments. I really want to learn how to play the harpsichord." He shapes his fantasy with his hands.

"Why don't you?"

"Because you have to have one to play it, and we don't."

"You should get one!" she urges.

"We aren't rich, and my papa doesn't like music anymore."

"Oh, okay. Well, you will have one someday."

"I hope so," he says confidently.

The rasp of metal wheels draws their attention, and looking around, Bart sees the source of the noise is a woman driving a horse-drawn wagon.

"I have to go," Adele says, her disappointment clear in her voice. "That is my mama."

"Okay, see you tomorrow." Bart walks Adele to the wagon, and they hug momentarily before she climbs up beside her mother. He waits for a few minutes, watching his new friend leave the park before heading home.

She thinks I am a good inventor!

CHAPTER
Two

1682 – Bart
18 Years Later

*T*he cobblestone streets smell of fresh flower arrangements and horse manure as Bart walks briskly on the sidewalk of Liston Road. Sweat glistens on his forehead, the only indication of his burning excitement for what awaits him only moments from now. Padua is busy on Saturday mornings. Markets across the city open up with homemade goods piled high as the eye can see. Half a century after the terrible economic depression, people have been enjoying the trade of goods again. Padua has always been a strong city, and is still one of the reasons Italy is seeing brighter days.

Pedrocchi Café is only about a thirty-minute walk from Bart's home, but today's crowded streets make the journey closer to an hour. Still, he arrives in ample time, and taking a deep breath, followed by a fast exhalation, he enters through the café's dark green door, admonishing himself: *Be brave.*

Once inside, he hangs his copper-toned doublet on the entry coat hanger and is about to survey the crowd when a man with a prominent nose wearing a prestigious white wig arrives at his side, hand outstretched. "Bartolomeo?"

Bart's eyes open wide with surprise. "Yes, sir." *This must be him!*

"So great to finally meet you! I am Andrea de' Medici of Florence and the Florentine Court. Have a seat with me?"

Bart follows Andrea across the café, peeling back his shirtsleeves so the cuffs are above his wrists, and they sit down. "It is good to meet you, Andrea," Bart says. "Having only conversed with you through a letter, this is proving to be a pleasure." His voice is higher pitched than usual, revealing his joy and nervousness in meeting with a man of such prestige and wealth in Florence.

"Agreed." Andrea's voice is deep but kind.

Andrea set up this meeting a few months ago, but didn't mention anything regarding its purpose. Bart doesn't care, though. Meeting with anyone from the Florentine Court is an honor, a dream.

"If I may ask," Bart begins, "why did you want to meet with me here? Wouldn't the studio be more fitting so you could see our collection?"

"Actually, Bart, I'm not here about the harpsichord collection."

"Okay." *What else could he possibly want to talk about?*

"I'm here only for you."

"But I am just an ordinary builder." *Why would he want to meet with me?* Bart thinks, his self-doubt beginning to question Andrea's motives.

"You are the inventor of the two-keyboard harpsichord, correct?"

"I am," Bart answers.

"What a beautiful instrument it is. My compositions sound wonderful on it, and it is an honor to meet you."

"It's my honor, truly, Andrea. Your compositions are so moving," Bart answers, and he cannot help his note of pride and confidence.

"Thank you, Bart, that means a lot coming from you. I mean it. Thank you."

Bart returns Andrea's smile, taking in the moment unfolding before him. He has only heard stories of this man who is renowned for his musical compositions and instrumental skills. He is a sign of hope and peace amid a world full of war.

A waitress appears and they order food.

When she is gone, Andrea says, "As amazing as your invention is, I still have something else I want to discuss. If that is fine by you?"

"Absolutely."

"I have spent my life composing music. I've always loved it and desired to create and share it with the world." Andrea speaks in an animated rush, then after a considering pause, he begins again, speaking more slowly. "However, my ideas have evolved and matured over time, but the instruments available have not. The harpsichord is beautiful, make no mistakes, but it no longer allows me to create the music I want to."

Frowning, Bart says, "I'm not sure I understand. It is complex and capable, is it not? The keyboard offers endless possibilities for musical composition."

"Yes! The keyboard is perfect, but it has become lacking in expression."

What is that supposed to mean?

As if he has read the thought in Bart's mind, Andrea continues. "When it is my intention to create a new melody and harmony, I am met with the same volume and speed at which I can play."

Catching on to Andrea's meaning, Bart says, "Do you want a quieter or louder harpsichord?"

"Both."

"We have both in stock at the studio."

Looking skeptical, Andrea says, "In the same instrument?"

"That isn't possible," Bart says, matter-of-factly.

"For now."

"Andrea—"

"You can call me Andy, please."

"Andy, the strings work harmoniously with the plucking mechanisms inside a harpsichord. One cannot change how hard or soft the strings are played without adjusting every pick inside the instrument."

"Exactly. That is where it is lacking in expression. The intensity of the tone of the melody should adjust according to the player's desire, not depend on its builder to adjust it."

Bart leaned back, crossing his arms now. "I don't think you want a harpsichord, then."

"Maybe not. But I know there is an instrument that can be made to suit what I have described to you."

"With a keyboard and strings like a harpsichord that adjusts the relative softness or loudness of the tones at the command of the one playing it?" he asks, feeling as though he is describing a fantasy.

"Exactly." Andy smiles.

"I don't know of anything like that."

"This is why I came to you. I believe you can create the instrument we are talking about."

"You want to hire me?" Bart's tone reflects his disbelief.

"Yes."

"To invent this—" Bart breaks off, and in his struggle to find the right words to convey his doubt in his skill to produce Andrea's vision, he gestures dramatically with his hands as if playing the harpsichord—"this instrument we are imagining?"

"Yes."

This is ridiculous. How could it be possible? "I'm not sure."

"Bartolomeo—"

"Call me Bart, please."

"Bart. I've played an instrument you built, and I can tell from the sound and craftsmanship that you are the one for this task. You have the ability to invent the instrument which will change music forever."

Bart, letting his doubt show on full display, looks at Andy.

"The compositions I have heard in my imagination, and the instrument upon which I play them are nothing short of marvelous. I have dreamed almost every night of being able to create new music, the kind people hear in their hearts and souls, not just their ears."

"I am fascinated by your ideas, I am. And thank you for the compliment. Where would this opportunity be exactly?"

"Florence."

Florence! That is more than two days' travel away.

"I would have to move," he says softly, more to himself than Andy.

"You would. However, Florence is the music capital of the world; you will fit in well there."

"I have always wondered what it would be like to live in Florence, but Padua is my home." Sitting back, Bart loosens his gaze, letting it drift, unseeing, through the café's windows.

"I understand. This is an especially beautiful city." Andy follows Bart's glance.

Bart looks at him. "Can I think about it?"

"I'll be in Padua for the next few days; I would like an answer before I leave."

Bart nods. "Where can I find you?"

"I'll be staying at Grand'Italia Inn."

They fall into a discussion of their successful careers once their meals are served. Bart has worked at a local instrument builder's shop for twelve years, becoming a highly skilled instrument builder. He is too humble to admit to his talent, but he is not surprised by Andy's compliments. He knows his craftsmanship is unmatched. What was once his dream is now his reality and has been for years, but every day still feels like the first. His energy and excitement for his work never fades.

Beginning his hour-long walk home after he and Andy have finished their meals, he nearly skips in his excitement, thinking of Adele. He can't wait to tell her!

CHAPTER
Three

Adele

*T*he fragrance of lavender and basil fills Adele's nostrils, offering a momentary escape from the discomfort inside her body. She has known for the past few days that something was different this time, but now she knows exactly why.

Adele loves working in her garden. It is a masterpiece, the envy of the entire neighborhood. Carefully, she pushes herself up and off the ground, freshly harvested herbs in hand, and heads into her pale-yellow colored home. Entering her kitchen, she is setting the basket holding her harvest on the kitchen counter when an anticipated knock at the door catches her attention.

Molly, she thinks, walking to the door, wiping her hands on her apron.

Molly comes over multiple times a week and every Saturday around midday. The visits are ritual and give them a chance to catch up on any local drama and air their complaints about married life.

"Took you long enough," Molly says by way of greeting. Her black hair is tied into a bun, and her dark eyes settle on Adele with sisterly love.

"Good to see you too," Adele says, letting her friend inside, and pulling her loose strands of vibrant blond hair behind her ear, revealing a handful of sunspots on her shoulders. A gift from the sun every fair-skinned person in Italy receives through the years.

Molly is carrying her usual armful of freshly baked bread that she will trade for the fresh produce Adele provides. The routine means that neither has to spend money at the market except for special occasions—a lesson learned from their parents.

"Oh. My. Gosh. Why so much lavender?" Molly exclaims when the aroma engulfs her.

"I'm sorry, but I have really been craving the smell of it the last few days. It helps ease my discomfort." Adele pointedly rubs her stomach, waiting for Molly to look, wanting her to notice.

But her friend is absorbed in unloading bread from her basket, and without so much as a side glance at Adele, she says, "What discomfort?"

Leaning further over the table, Adele continues massaging her stomach area and when that fails to get Molly's attention, she clears her throat.

Now, when Molly finally looks at her, she gasps, and laying a hand on her heart, she says, "The sun shining through the window makes it hard to see, but I think I see a bump!"

Adele huffs. "There is no bump yet."

Molly rushes to her, tears welling in her eyes. "Oh, Adele. I'm so happy for you!"

"Thank you," Adele says before stepping out of their embrace.

"Does this time feel different? I don't mean to change the mood," Molly adds hastily, "but you know I'm a worrier." Sympathy warms Molly's expression. The two women have been best friends since childhood.

"It does. I think I am at least eight weeks along now."

"Eight weeks! And you're just now telling me?"

"I wanted to be sure. I haven't even told Bart yet."

"Adele!"

"I can't disappoint him again."

"You would never disappoint Bart. He loves you in a way I have never seen or experienced."

"I know that, but still. We've tried for twelve years, and we are both almost thirty. Each time I've been pregnant, it has ended in devastation."

"But this time is different!" Molly seizes Adele's hands.

"Yes, it is!" Wanting to believe in her friend's reassurance, Adele agrees, but with a heartiness she doesn't quite feel.

"I am so excited for you. I've prayed endlessly for this baby, you know that, and the feeling inside me is indescribable right now."

"I know you have, Molly, and I am beyond grateful." A wave of love for her friend sweeps over her. "You're one of the biggest reasons I can still have hope."

They turn to the work at hand, sorting baked goods and vegetables, and their talk is lighthearted and broken by giggles.

"So, how are Marco and Sammy?" Adele asks, when they have finished their weekly trade session.

"Ugh. Don't get me started on Marco. He is as unhelpful and distant as ever. Sammy is doing well, although his ten-year age is starting to show itself a bit. He can be a mouthy child."

"Just like his mama."

"Watch it," Molly says jokingly, glaring sidelong at Adele. Adele sticks her tongue out at Molly while letting her finish talking. "I don't know what to do about Marco. All he ever does is work, and when he does come home, he expects me to do everything."

"Caring for the house is your job, though, Molly," Adele says with a reminding tone.

"I know. It's not being a wife and mother that bothers me. It's feeling alone even though I'm married that does."

She puts her hand on Molly's arm, looking into her eyes reassuringly "I'm sorry, Molly. I still pray every day for your relationship. It will improve, I believe it."

"Thank you. I guess I look at your marriage with Bart and try to compare Marco and myself to you." With big eyes, revealing her discomfort in being too serious, Molly adds, "Which makes me feel especially discouraged!"

"Molly, I may not complain about my marriage much, but trust me, it's not perfect."

"Only someone in a perfect relationship would say that." Molly laughs.

Adele can't help but join her. Her relationship with Bart *is* near perfect, though she would never tell her friend so. She would never hurt Molly that way. It would be unhelpful. Neither will she tell Molly that after every miscarriage, she and Bart have found a greater love for each other. It's the only way they have made it through each time, made them willing to try again.

"When are you going to tell him?" Molly drops her glance to Adele's still flat belly.

She's changing the subject, and Adele goes along. "As soon as he comes home. He is meeting with a famous music composer from Florence downtown."

"So soon! Well, I will gather up my groceries and get out of here. You'll need some time alone before having the conversation. It'll be emotional."

"Thanks, like I need more to be nervous about," Adele says.

"All happy emotions and tears of joy," Molly says encouragingly.

Adele smiles at her flamboyant friend, who never fails to make every situation worthy of a laugh. "I love you, Molly." They walk out of the kitchen, Molly's dark green gown fluttering with each step.

"I love you too, Adele. I am so happy for you! See you in a few days for lunch." They embrace a final time, and Adele notices before closing the door that Molly wipes a tear from her cheek. Adele's own throat is tight with tears; she is grateful for Molly's support but still anxious over giving Bart her news.

She is back in the garden when less than an hour later she hears the sound of a whistle dancing in the air and knows Bart is home. *It's a happy tune,* she thinks. *His meeting went well!* Leaving her herb-cutting task behind her, Adele rushes in through the back door toward Bart as he enters the front of the house. "Honey!" she cries.

"Hi, b—babe!" He stutters a bit, surprised by her excitement.

After a hug and kiss, Adele asks, "How did the meeting go?" already sure of the answer.

"It was incredible to meet a composer from the Florentine Court! His name is Andy, and you will *never* believe what he wanted to speak to me about."

Bart is wide eyed, elated in a way Adele has not seen for a while. "What?" she demands, looking up at him. "Tell me."

"It's crazy but he has this idea for an instrument like a harpsi-chord—" Bart begins to pace their front room and, pausing beside their harpsichord illuminated by the sun gleaming from the nearest window, he says—"but it will play both soft *and* loud."

"Piano and forte?"

"Exactly!"

"What is so crazy about that?" Adele asks him. She's curious. It seems reasonable to her, not that she knows so much about musical instruments.

"It doesn't exist. An instrument can't adjust volume without being internally remodeled."

"Oh," she says.

"Well, not yet, I mean." Bart hesitates, then striding over to Adele he takes both of her hands. "He wants *me* to invent it."

Adele drops her jaw, and her wide eyes match his now. "You can't be serious." Memories of Bart telling her his dreams of being an inventor as a child come rushing back to her mind.

"I am," Bart says proudly.

"Oh, Bart, this is so incredible!"

"We have only a few days to decide if we want to take the opportunity."

"What is there to decide? This is your dream!"

"I'll have to work in Florence."

Her stomach drops, and her face betrays her before she can hide her sudden disappointment.

"I know, Adele," Bart says, reading her expression. "I feel the same."

She pulls away. "Um, let me think for a second." Seating herself in the nearest chair, she works to quell her apprehension. How can she agree given her condition? But how can she not? Even she knew such opportunities as this were rare. She meets Bart's anxious glance. "I think you should accept."

"Wait. Really? How are you so sure?"

By his expression, Adele thinks he is the one who is more anxious now. "It's scary," she says, "but the chance to create something
so innovative may never come again. You can't pass it up."

"That is true." Sitting down in an adjacent armchair, Bart stares
at the floor.

"What is wrong? Why are you doubting it?" Adele leans forward,
cupping her husband's forearm.

"I don't know exactly, except it's someone else's idea, not mine."
Bart meets Adele's glance.

"What is?" she asks.

"The idea for the instrument. It's someone else's vision. I'm not
sure I want to invent something I didn't think of first."

"Are you interested in the idea?"

"Yes, absolutely!"

"Think you can do it?"

She notices a slight blush of pride on Bart's cheeks before he
says, "Definitely."

"Then, who cares if you thought of it first? You don't have to
have the original idea to be the one to make it a reality." She watches
as Bart's expression turns from indecisiveness to confidence. A
beautiful transformation.

"I can do that. Moving is going to be so hard, though."

"We can take care of everything later and as it comes to pass.
Our lives are about to change drastically anyway," she says, and she
cannot keep her eager delight from showing in her voice any more
than she can stop herself from flattening her palm over her stomach.

"What do you mean?" Bart leans toward her, his glance resting
on her hand.

Taking a deep breath, she looks into her husband's eyes. "I'm
pregnant."

CHAPTER
four

Bart

*T*he harpsichord sings off-key as Bart takes his time tuning its long brass strings individually and precisely. It is only spring, and he has already hand-built two instruments; this is his third. The wood he selected, dark cherry, is sanded and oiled to his high expectations. The soundboard projects the strings' vibrations to the perfect volume requested by its buyer, to whom it will soon be delivered.

"So, you are moving?" Marco asks, breaking the momentary silence inside Bart's workshop at the harpsichord studio.

"I guess so. I'm confirming it with Andy tomorrow," Bart answers, keeping his attention on the instrument. Not having to look at Marco makes it easier to talk about it. Although they aren't as close now as adults, they have been friends for the entirety of their lives, and the fact that he's leaving is difficult.

"I am so happy for you, Bart, but I also don't know what I'll do without you." Marco seems to read Bart's mind.

"Marco, I feel the same. But remember, you have Molly and Sammy."

"I know. I know. I feel bad for saying this, but I feel closer to you than my wife or son."

Hearing this from Marco doesn't surprise Bart, but it still makes his heart heavy. "What is bothering you, Marco?" he asks, turning his attention to his friend, sensing there is something more to it.

"You're moving away, and I'm just being emotional, is all. Sorry." Marco looks toward the windows on his left, highlighting his bushy eyebrows and clay-red shirt.

"It can't just be that. You've been distant for a while now." Bart eyes his friend intently until Marco meets his gaze again.

"I am unhappy," he says simply.

"I'm so sorry, Marco. Do you know how come?" Again, his friend's words do not surprise him.

"I don't know exactly. Every day I wake up, I can't stop thinking about how I wish my life were different."

"Different, how?"

"I feel like I'm still trying to live up to my father's expectations, even though he has been gone for years. I started working in the leather shop when I was nine, then inherited it when I turned eighteen, and I hate every day of my life because of the stupid business. You already know the story."

"I knew you didn't love working in the leather business, but I didn't realize it made you miserable."

"Well, it does. And now I have a family to care for, so I'm stuck with it forever."

"Not necessarily. You can find something else. You're a brilliant man. Ever since school, you've always been a genius."

"Yeah, right. Besides, I've never had the chance to try anything else, so I have no clue what I *actually* want to do."

"I am so sorry, Marco." Bart repeats his apology. "I really am. All these years I should have been a better friend."

"What? It's not your fault, Bart. No person's life is fair. I just needed to complain for a minute, but I'm fine."

"You sure?"

"Absolutely."

Bart doesn't know whether to believe him or not. "I have more news," Bart says, after a pause. He bends over the harpsichord's soundboard again.

"Yeah, what is it?" Marco asks.

"Adele and I are having a baby." He glances up at Marco, and noting his expression that mixes elements of both excitement and fear, he says, "Adele can tell something is different from the others this time."

"I am so happy for you!" Marco says, looking relieved and resting a hand on the edge of the instrument. "So, you're having a baby *and* moving cities?"

"Yes."

"Your life is being completely shaken up."

"That it is. Part of the reason we decided for me to take the new job and move is because our lives were already going to be changing, so why not change all at once?"

"Sounds like something two crazy people like yourselves would ask." Marco and Bart share a brief laugh followed by an abrupt silence that begins to feel awkward. Marco breaks it. "So, did she say how she knows this time is different? Sorry for asking, but—"

"It's fine, Marco. Trust me, I was really afraid, too. Each miscarriage we've endured is harder than the last. But she says her *whole body* feels different than with the previous pregnancies, and she is past eight weeks."

"Okay."

"It is her body, so she knows. Honestly, even I feel different this time. We both have confidence and faith like we've never had before."

"Okay. I believe this time will be different, too. You've convinced me."

"Thank you, Marco," Bart says as they embrace each other.

"So, will the baby be born here or in Florence?"

"Florence. We want our child to have and know just one home."

"Good idea. When are you planning to move?"

"In one month from tomorrow, mid-May."

"Oh. That's fast."

"It will be here before we know it."

The two friends reminisce, resurrecting memories from their childhood for almost an hour before Marco leaves. Bart finishes tuning the harpsichord, and he's well satisfied with its sound when he finally wraps up his work for the day and sets out for home, looking forward to spending the remainder of the weekend with the love of his life.

His route takes him along the same sidewalk he and Adele took to the park after each school day. A new generation of owners operates the beautiful brick-and-rock storefronts, but they have carried on the traditions of the old owners. Petunias and begonias of all colors—pink being the city's favorite—overtake the streets with their splendor, showcasing Padua's generous and lively heart, the same heart that keeps the city strong and successful and ever more beautiful.

Passing the church—the Basilica of St. Anthony—where he and Adele were married twelve years ago, Bart smiles. Even still, to this day, a host of welcome memories flood his mind. *The best day of my life, spent with the best part of my life!*

Both Adele and Bart grew up with the church being a huge influence in their lives, as most citizens in the country of Italy did. Their faith has become their own now, proud members of the church just like their parents were.

As he crosses the rock bridge, which takes him out of the city's center, he stops to admire the fish in the canal below. The wildflowers along the edge of the water offer them a place to hide, but with the sun still high in the sky, they're clearly visible from where he stands watching. He waves a greeting to a man and woman traveling through the city by canoe as they pass under the bridge.

"Delightful day today!" they call out.

While he will always treasure Padua's loveliness and the memories of a life he has built here, what he will miss most is undeniably the people. They are of great kindness, willing to support one another through anything. In all the years he and Adele have spent trying to have a baby, they have never felt alone. The community is the sort that quickly embraces its people and walks with them through their trials. Bart and Adele have both participated in and received the gift of being citizens of Padua.

He smiles when, upon entering his house, he finds Adele with her nose buried in a freshly picked bouquet of lavender, finding comfort in its scent. Watching her, he can't help but admire her glow and be grateful that she is his wife.

"I love you," he says, approaching her.

Lifting her head, she says softly, "I love you, too."

Bart takes her in his arms, and laying aside the lavender, she nestles against him. "Everything is about to change," she says, and Bart detects an edge of anxiety in her tone.

"I know." He smooths his hand over her back, wanting to comfort her. "Into all good things, though."

"I'm scared," she whispers against his chest.

"Me too," he says, and they stand quietly, allowing the silence, taking strength from one another.

CHAPTER
five

Adele
Five Weeks Later

*T*he sun is high in the sky when the filtered light gently wakes Adele. It is late to rise for her. She thinks there is something different about sunrise in Florence compared to Padua, or at least that is what she blames for her failure to maintain her usual early wake-up schedule. Bart refuses to wake her from her slumber. He is adamant about Adele sleeping for as long as her body wants—for the baby's health, of course.

Lying still for a moment longer, she remembers that today marks the start of the second week they have lived in Florence, and so far, since their arrival here Adele's only feeling is her longing for home. Pushing it aside, she crawls out of bed, reaching toward the sky in a big stretch, and yawns only to immediately sit back down and hold her stomach with both hands. It has been an endless challenge to discern the difference between the healthy pregnancy aches from the memories of cramps that came with miscarriage. She has never reached fourteen weeks of pregnancy before, so every twinge going forward is new to her. Even with the doctor's assurance that some discomfort is entirely natural, she is still afraid.

She takes a few deep breaths, and telling herself she's fine, she leaves the bedroom and heads to the kitchen. She opens the pantry cabinet, finds the empty shelves, and sighs. She will have to go shopping.

I miss my garden.

The local market is only a short walk from home, so she changes into her day clothes—a cream-colored smock and brown surcoat over her gown—and steps out into the lively Florence air full of horses clicking, shouts from the neighboring city street, and the smell of fresh pizza dough rising. The only thing missing is the hint of lavender.

The walkway from her terracotta-colored front door to the sidewalk is bare, with only dirt and rocks. *A canvas waiting for its artist to do her work!* Wildflower garden beds and colorful border ideas fill her creative mind as she walks at a steady pace to the market.

Spotting a woman sweeping her front porch, she waves and calls out to her. "Good morning!" she shouts with a friendly smile.

The woman only glares back at her as if she was a nuisance.

"I'm glad we aren't neighbors," Adele mutters under her breath. Refusing to return the woman's glare, she smiles even bigger than before, ending it with a dramatic humph.

As she nears the market, the aroma of yeast bread rising grows stronger as does a more familiar smell.

Basil! The herb's name sings in her brain.

Hurrying her steps, she follows her nose to a fresh herb stand.

"Good morning, ma'am." A short, older man addresses her from the side of the little wooden cart.

"Good morning! You weren't here Saturday," she says.

"I was, but you've got to be here early on the weekend. I sell out fast."

Adele inhales deeply the fragrance of the herbs, satisfying her homesickness for a moment. "I'll take a stem of each, please."

"Perfect," the older man says and begins wrapping each of the stems together with burlap string. When he finishes, he adds a bouquet of daisies to her stuffed bag.

"I'm sorry, I don't want any flowers today," she says.

"They are my gift to you. Enjoy!"

"Oh, well, thank you so much." Impulsively, she hugs him, and waving goodbye, she walks to a bread cart that catches her attention. At first glance, she sees Molly standing beside it with her lengthy, black hair, but when the woman turns around, of course it isn't Molly. Adele feels a pang of sadness. *I miss Molly.*

"How can I help you?" the woman asks. Her jawline is so sharp it could slice the bread, Adele thinks.

"I'll take two loaves," she says, pointing to the bread with seeds covering the top.

Wrapping Adele's purchase, she says, "I have never seen you here before. New to Florence?" Her eyes on Adele are curious.

"Yes, this is our second week in Florence." Adele tucks the bread into her satchel, next to the herbs from earlier. "We moved from Padua. My husband was offered a job here."

"Interesting. What kind of job?"

"He works at the music hall downtown. He is a harpsichord builder, and they asked him to come work for them."

"He must be good then. They only take the finest instrument builders and musicians there."

"He is very skilled and has loved working with instruments since he was a kid," Adele says with pride.

"Any children?" she asks flatly.

"No, we have no children yet. One on the way, though," Adele says with a happy chuckle.

The woman's eyes widen. "You are a woman of decent age, and you have yet to have children?"

"Excuse me?" Adele takes a step back.

"No offense, but you look too old to be having your *first* baby." The woman's voice is emotionless.

"You don't know anything about me."

"I'm surprised your husband is still with you."

Adele feels the heat of her anger bleed from her neck onto her face. *How dare she speak to me in this way?* "Why would he leave me?" she asks, forcing herself to speak calmly. She is not easily angered, but something about this woman's tone is triggering every nerve inside of her.

"Well, I doubt waiting until your current age was *his* idea. Most men would have left you for a woman who can give him children, deeming you useless."

"I'm not a cow, bitch!" Adele shouts more loudly than she means to. Embarrassment for using such a demeaning word in public rushes through her but doesn't reduce her anger.

The woman appears unruffled. "That is what we are to men, dear. We are tools that produce their offspring. It's our only purpose."

"I do not envy your marriage then, if that's how it is for you. Please stay out of my business because my marriage is just fine."

"Is it?"

"Yes. Even if I were *never* to have children, my husband and I would be together because we love each other."

The woman scoffs. "Yeah, right. You don't actually believe that, do you?"

"Who do you think you are?" she asks with a look of disgust.

"I am a woman who has been at the mercy of men my whole life. Considered useless and unfit to be a wife. I am saying this to you for your own good."

"I appreciate the gesture but not the bitterness. I best be on my way," Adele says. She feels the woman's gaze drilling her back as she leaves the market. The encounter has dampened her spirits, and she stops only to pick up some tomatoes and peppers before heading home. Arriving there, rather than going inside, she sits on a stone front step. She can't stop thinking of what the woman at the market said. Was it true? Would Bart stop loving her if she didn't give him a baby?

The question screams inside of her. She has never had any reason to think otherwise until now. And now another rises to scorch the walls of her brain. Suppose she loses this baby too? Will it be the end of his patience with her? A cloud of worry grows behind her eyes. The woman's cruel words have struck a nerve inside her, seeming to have uncovered many of the fears she has managed to subdue and hide away over the years. A woman with no husband and no children really is worthless. No jobs exist for such women. She couldn't even own property to grow food to live.

I hate Florence.

The bitter thought rises in her mind. Tears burn in her eyes. The combined weight of all that has happened, moving to a new city, leaving behind her best friend, and now the fear of becoming worthless, falls over her, and it is a struggle to stand, requiring all of her strength. But just as she is about to go inside and begin preparing dinner, she hears a familiar song, whistled through the lips of the man she loves. Peering down the street, she sees him, walking toward her, wearing a smile on his face. "He is home," she whispers to herself.

CHAPTER
Six

1682 – Bart
The Same Day

*L*eaving Adele to her sleep, Bart quietly closes the front door, a small loaf of bread for lunch tucked under one arm. The music hall of the Florentine Court, his still-new workplace, is almost an hour's walk from home. It's a longer walk than he is used to, but he will soon adjust.

His morning routine is his favorite part of living in Florence so far. Every morning, on his arrival at his workshop in the back of the music hall, he has the opportunity to meet with any number of talented musicians and composers. Andy included.

"Good morning, Bart!" Andy's greeting is filled with his upbeat energy.

"Good morning, Andy!" he replies.

"A few of us are having tea and breakfast in a moment. Care to join?"

"Absolutely," he gladly accepts the invitation.

Although it is only the beginning of the second week of working for Andy, Bart's fear of not fitting in has already faded. His dream of being an inventor is not only being realized but surpassed in terms of the delightful people he works with daily.

He drops his lunch on the cabinet top in his workshop and then heads quickly to the café across the street to meet with Andy and the other musicians. When he arrives, the group of five is discussing their newest arrangement—testing the violin skills of the youngest man at the table: Frank.

"You've written the piece in the most difficult key and in a time signature of torture," Frank complains.

"But once you master it, you will go down in history for playing one of the most beautiful pieces of music," Andy says to encourage Frank.

"If I can master it," Frank says.

"You will," Antonio says, patting Frank on his back.

As Bart takes a seat among them, Antonio addresses him. "How are you liking your workspace?" He is an older man of great height but even greater achievements. Florence might not be the music capital of the world today if it weren't for him.

Bart is flattered by his attention. "I like it a lot. Plenty of room and all the tools I should need."

"Good."

"Thank you again," Bart says—including Andy in his words of gratitude—"for the opportunity to create something potentially remarkable."

"You are welcome. And thank you for accepting. We are honored to have you here. We know your craftsmanship is unmatched."

Bart smiles, feeling the swell of pride. He thinks it is going to be hard to stay humble around these people.

Rocco, another man at the table with a long, dark beard, asks, "How are you and your family adjusting to life in Florence?"

"My wife and I love it here so far. Of course, we miss home, but everyone has made us feel so welcome here."

"Glad to hear that. And your children?" Rocco asks.

"We have no children yet."

"Oh, I'm sorry." Rocco quickly apologizes.

"There is no need. We have a baby on the way!"

"Congratulations!" everyone at the table says.

"Thank you." Bart feels his face warm.

"Well, boys, thanks for breakfast; I'm going to get on with my day," Antonio says, standing up from the table, which prompts the others to do the same.

When Bart arrives back at his new shop, he takes a moment to admire it. The empty space boldly awaits his creativity to fill it with what only exists in his imagination—for now.

Cypress wood for the soundboard.

Maple wood for the body of the instrument. The most stunning grains, he thinks.

Tung oil to make his invention shine.

The only object in the room presently—other than a full wall lined with tools—is a stool and an easel with a large blank canvas. Wandering to the stool, he sits and focuses on the canvas. In the last week, his ideas have gelled. He will begin with an outline of a traditional harpsichord, three legs, a large body shaped to match the length of the strings, and an adjustable height cover. And then, through a series of trial-and-error sketches, he will see ways to expand on the basic drawing until finally he will have invented an entirely new instrument. Satisfied with his plan, Bart picks up the pencil, and leaning in close to the canvas, he focuses his eyes on his hand and lets his imagination lead its movement.

Afternoons in Florence seem to Bart to arrive faster than in Padua, or maybe all the energy from so much change is moving time more quickly. Despite wanting to spend all night at his shop cultivating ideas, he leaves his mostly empty workshop and heads home. The walk is beautiful but not the same as Padua. Home. Nothing he walks past offers memories; no architecture holds a story—that he would know—and no storefront business provides the same kind of friendly smiles he is used to. But, he assures himself, this will feel like home eventually. Coming within sight of his house, he sees Adele waiting for him on the front steps, and his heart jumps inside his chest. Even though they've been married for over a decade, her bright eyes and beauty still captivates him. On approaching her, he notices her solemn face.

"What's wrong, my love?" he asks.

"How was your day at the shop?" she says, ignoring his question.

"It was so good! I love it so far, and everyone is still beyond welcoming and kind."

Although Adele smiles, and says she's glad for him, Bart catches the subtle roll of her eyes. Clearly, something is troubling her.

"Are you okay?" he asks her, keeping her gaze.

"I'm fine," she says, standing up and turning to go inside. "I went shopping today, so we will have some fresh pasta with basil pesto for dinner."

Bart follows her, shutting the door behind them. "I know something is wrong. Are you going to tell me?"

She says over her shoulder, "You don't want to know."

"Seriously, Adele? You know better."

"Fine." She sets her produce-filled satchel on the counter with a huff. "My day was ruined by a rude lady at the market."

"Oh no. I'm sorry. How so?" he asks, helping unpack the groceries.

When Adele's mouth quivers, and she squeezes her eyes to withhold tears, Bart quickly wraps her in his arms and feels her burrowing against him.

"She made me feel like I am a bad person for not having a child before now."

"Oh, baby. Her words mean nothing." Bart is quick to offer comfort.

"I know. She doesn't even know me and our situation at all, yet she still made me feel terrible."

"I'm so sorry." He tightens his embrace, feeling protective of his wife.

"She also said that a woman's only purpose is to have children, and that she was surprised we were still married," Adele says, her voice breaking.

Leaning a little away, he says, "That is so wrong. I can't believe she said that."

"I know!" Adele meets his gaze and says with a surprise chuckle, "God, she was such a bitch."

"Adele!" Bart exclaims, laughing himself. "That is not like you."

"What? Don't you agree?"

You can't be a nice guy here, he reminds himself. "Yes, definitely. She is a bitch. If I'd been there, I would not have let her even talk to you. She couldn't be more wrong!"

"Thank you," Adele says, and stepping back into his embrace, she hugs him tightly even as she wipes away a couple of tears. They share another laugh at themselves. "Is it true, though?" she asks a few moments later, her head against his chest.

"Is what true?" he asks.

"Have you thought of leaving me for a woman who could give you children?"

Bart pulls away and looks deep into Adele's eyes. "Never once. Not even for a moment."

"Really?"

"Adele. I am with you because I love you."

"Even if..."

"Even if what?"

"Even if our baby now... you know. What if it happens again?"

"Don't say that. Our baby is healthy. You've said many times that everything feels different, and the doctor is confident, too."

"But what if..."

"I am going to be your husband no matter what. I'm going to love you no matter what. I'm going to stand right here by your side no matter what. This is love. This is us."

"I know you want to be a father with all your heart, and I've failed."

"You want to be a mother too. We both want to be parents. We are in this together. You understand that, right?"

Adele nods. "I do. I just needed to be reminded."

Bart pulls her in close again, relishing the feel of her in his arms. He imagines their hearts beating in unison. Resting his chin on the crown of her head, he says, "What the lady said has made you question our relationship, but her words were untrue. Maybe it's true for her situation and her experiences. But she is not us. We're special, Adele, and our love is resilient. Look at what we have been through."

"I know. I'm sorry for questioning."

"Sometimes life makes us question. But promise me, you'll always bring your questions and insecurities to me. I promise to bring mine to you."

Adele smiles, her eyes still shiny with tears, but her solemn face is gone, replaced by an expression of peace. "I promise."

Bart kisses her forehead, and he thinks as they prepare their evening meal together that while the path ahead of them is long, their relationship is strong. Strong enough to endure whatever trials will come. Dreams aren't realized, he thinks, without facing some obstacles along the way. He can only pray they will not be like mountains of the sort that make it impossible to get through.

CHAPTER
Seven

1683 – Adele
Seven Months Later

Dear Molly,

Our baby girl is healthy and already growing like a weed. She is six weeks old now and has almost no hair. Even though bald, she is the most beautiful little thing I have ever seen. She still sleeps most of the time, but when she is awake, it seems all she does is smile. When she cries, all I have to do is lay her head on my chest, pressed against my heart, and she calms down immediately. I have to do so multiple times at night, but each time is a pleasure. I know now why I have always wanted to be a mother; my love has outgrown what I ever thought possible. She is our little miracle, and we named her Mira, but we have already nicknamed her

Cuori because of her desire to be close to a heartbeat.

I miss you, Molly. Life in Florence has been difficult for me. I have yet to make any friends, only a few acquaintances in a matter of six months. On the other hand, Bart has managed to make many good friends, for which I am glad, but if I am completely honest, I am also a bit jealous. I am proud of him, though; he is so smart and never ceases to amaze me. His time here is spent mainly at his shop, inventing the instrument that can play both soft and loud. I don't think it will be much longer before he finishes it. Besides his work, he makes an excellent father. The way his eyes light up when he sees Cuori melts my heart. My love for him has surpassed what I thought possible as well.

How are you doing? Selling a lot of baked goods? And how are Marco and Sammy? I cannot wait to hear from you. I love you, Molly.

Your dearest friend,
Adele

Adele folds the handwritten letter carefully three ways and stuffs it into an envelope, thinking she'll drop it off this afternoon to the mercantile company, then she takes a moment to admire her miracle. Cuori breathes softly and steadily as she sleeps. Carefully lifting the linen-stuffed cradle, Adele carries it into the backyard, which was bare ground only months ago—like the front yard— but is now a beautiful garden in progress. Of course, two rows of lavender are the oldest plants in the garden and, therefore, command the most attention from her. The fragrance is still a delight to her senses even after pregnancy.

She gently sits Cuori at the edge of the garden in the shade as she lowers to her knees so she can begin turning the soil, weeding, and watering. Gardening is Adele's form of art, her way of creating a living masterpiece, unpredictable but influenced by proper care. The morning sun will soon fade to the more intense heat and humidity of midday, at which time she will have finished here and move on to the rest of her daily chores.

Later in the afternoon, Adele finally decides to send off Molly's letter. The walk to the city's heart is familiar to her now. She recognizes each house and business storefront as she walks by, smiling and waving at each of her neighbors whom she has become fairly acquainted with.

The mercantile company office is near a park. She thinks how after mailing her letter she would like to go there. The little girl inside of her yearns for the carefree atmosphere, but the adult in her says it's silly, that Cuori is much too young to enjoy the experience and she would only be going for herself. But on leaving the mercantile, she is overcome with an urge to visit the park after all, and although others might judge her, she decides she will take the chance. How can it hurt?

On her arrival, though, she finds the place uncommonly busy, prompting her to leave immediately.

Just as she turns to go home, she hears a woman shout, "There is an open seat beside me!"

Adele glances at the lady. She has long, wavy brown hair, and is wearing a lovely purple gown. "Are you talking to me?" she asks the woman.

"Yes. Come and sit down," the woman says. Her skin is olive-toned and glowing.

"Thank you. I'm Adele," she adds as she props Cuori, still in her small cradle, on her lap.

"You're welcome; happy to. It's much busier here than usual. I'm Anna."

Adele notices a cradle on the ground beside Anna, holding a baby, too. With a curious smile, she asks, "And who is this doll?"

"This is Luca! He is twelve weeks old now."

"He is precious," Adele says, admiringly. "This is Mira. She is just six weeks old. Her nickname is Cuori." Adele beams with pride.

"What a gorgeous name. She even looks like a miracle." Anna oohs and aahs over Cuori, making Adele smile both inside and out. "Do you come to the park often?" she asks.

"This is my first time bringing Cuori. I wanted to see what it was like since I'm sure this will soon be her favorite place. The park where I'm from was always mine as a child."

"Me too! I would spend hours after school on the swings. A benefit to living in the city. I have been bringing Luca here most afternoons. It gets us out of the house," Anna says, making a disgusted face. "I do not enjoy housework."

"You and me both." Adele chuckles.

"You're not from Florence?"

"No, my husband and I moved here this Spring."

"What does your husband do?" Anna asks.

"Bart works at the music hall downtown." She searches for the right words but comes up short. *Is he an inventor now, or still a builder?* She wonders. "He builds instruments there," she decides.

"How interesting. Is he a musician?"

"He can certainly play the harpsichord and guitar, but he is a builder by heart. He loves to put all the little pieces together to create a beautiful instrument."

"How fascinating," Anna says.

"And your husband?"

"Dario is a winemaker at Paggiopiano Winery, on the edge of the city. He manages a small team there."

"How interesting! How long has he done that?"

"Since he was a teenager. He learned winemaking from his father, who also worked at Paggiopiano Winery."

"That is impressive."

"Thank you. I am proud of him. He takes good care of us and is a good papa for Luca." She leans down to rock her baby ever-so-softly.

An awkward silence fills the air around them for a moment. It doesn't last long when Anna asks, "So what is your story?"

Adele is quickly struck with a blank mind. "My story?"

"Yeah! Your daughter's name means "miracle." Surely that comes with a story, right?" Anna's glance was curious but in a thoughtful way.

Adele warmed to her. "It does come with a story, a long one. Are you sure you want to hear it?" She laughs.

Anna sweeps her gaze over the park. "I have all afternoon."

Adele has never been asked such an intimidating yet alluring question. She had only lived in Padua up until now, and essentially everyone there already knew her. Her thoughts churned with ideas of how to answer. She plays with the question for a moment in her mind before settling on one of countless memories to begin with.

"I met my husband when we were both nine years old," Adele begins, and she goes on, describing how the friendship grew, how she and Bart had fallen in love and married. She mentions her mother and father, but then, feeling as if she is sounding too self-absorbed, she pauses.

"You and your mother were close?" Anna asks.

Gratified by Anna's attention, Adele says, "Yes, absolutely. She always loved me for me. I never felt trapped inside expectations with her like I did with my father."

"Your father had a lot of expectations?"

Adele fake gasps. "Let's just say he did not like that I didn't fit the image of a 'normal girl' my age."

"What do you mean?"

Adele hesitated, unsure how much she wanted to reveal. "I didn't like wearing dresses, I would get dirty from playing with the boys at the park, and I was always too vocal and opinionated."

Anna laughs. "You didn't fit the city girl image."

Adele laughs shortly, too, then more soberly, she says, "He died two years ago, but even up to his last day on earth, he made sure to let me know he was disappointed in me."

"You were a bold girl. He must have feared society would reject you," Anna says. She smiles sympathetically and her dimples show.

"I know he did. I have lost most of that boldness, though. As a little kid, you don't know what to fear. As an adult, you don't know what *not* to fear."

"So true. What did your father have to be disappointed about in you as an adult? If I can ask?"

Anna's gaze on Adele is gentle, and steady in a way that Adele finds reassuring. She can trust Anna, she thinks. "He thought Bart and I should have had a baby long before now."

"Cuori is your first child?"

"Yes."

"How old are you?"

"Twenty-nine."

"That is definitely later than most women start," Anna says, eyeing Adele with curiosity. "It wasn't by choice?" Her question speaks to society's expectations of women.

"I had six miscarriages before I had her, one almost every year in the last twelve years." Adele has confided her struggle to bear a child only a handful of times, and hearing it now makes something in her heart burst, causing a flood of tears.

"Oh, Adele. I am so very sorry." Anna shifts closer to Adele and rests her hand on Adele's forearm.

She collects herself rather quickly, fearing being noticed by strangers around them. "I never told my father about them because I was scared he would be madder at me than he already was."

"Did your mother know?"

"She died when I was fifteen. A year before I was married."

"I'm sorry," Anna says again, and her eyes glimmer with her own tears. "That must have been so hard for you."

"I think the boldness I had as a girl came from my mother and left with her because it was after she passed that my father's criticism began to eat away at my confidence."

"I think that is probably true for me, also. I lost my mother too."

"Oh, Anna. I'm so sorry." Adele pats Anna's hand, thinking it's no wonder that Anna is so understanding.

"I remember how I felt alone, even though I was surrounded by my entire family. A mother is a pillar inside our hearts, and when she's gone, every heartbeat for the rest of our lives is changed," Anna says, whispering at the end.

"I love that, Anna. How beautiful." Adele clears her throat. "I really enjoy talking to you. I'm sorry for rambling on about myself for so long."

"I needed this today, Adele. I loved hearing about your life. We have to meet again soon. I can see us being good friends."

"Me too." Adele smiles, her heart glowing inside her chest. "How old are you?"

"I am twenty."

Adele's eyes widen. She is much younger than Adele would have guessed. "I have to hear your story as well someday."

"Yes! Be prepared. It is a long one, too." They both laugh and then hug.

Before going their separate ways, Adele gives Anna directions to her home, and they set a lunch date.

Adele's feet feel lighter on leaving the park. She barely registers the snug weight of Cuori fast asleep in the basket she carries at her side. She has missed Molly for months now and was starting to believe she would never make a friend again. And to think, she almost didn't go to the park!

CHAPTER
Eight

Bart

*T*he air vibrates and bends to the will of the violin as Frank practices his solo piece. The gentle yet bold music never fails to entertain Bart's ears each day when he arrives at his shop. He waves at Frank as he passes by. Frank is thoroughly engrossed in reading the written music as he plays but catches a glimpse of Bart passing. Frank lifts the bow from the violin strings, causing an immediate silence to consume the room.

"Good morning, Bart!" Frank shouts with a big smile on his face.

"Morning!" Bart shouts back across the music hall auditorium.

Frank is seated on the stage in the colossal room, which is fitted with every instrument needed for an orchestra. The floor space can accommodate a thousand chairs, which is intimidating even when empty. Frank picks up where he left off after greeting Bart, and Bart continues down the hallway leading to his smaller but much more comfortable workspace.

Before he walks through the doorway, he recognizes Andy's shoulders. He is standing in the middle of the room.

"Andy. Beautiful day, isn't it?"

Andy turns slowly with a smooth motion. He wears his white wig proudly and perhaps is one of the very few men who actually look good in one. "It is indeed," he says with his deep, confident voice.

Bart sets his loaf of bread on the shelf near the door, then turns and faces Andy. "Ready to see what I've come up with this week?"

"Of course. I am tempted each day to stop by, but I know I would become a hindrance, a nuisance at best."

Bart laughs. "You could never be a nuisance, Andy," he says, even as he is grateful that Andy gives him his space.

They walk to the other side of the room, passing by a small pile of lumber being sanded as smooth as an ancient stone collected from a riverbed, waiting to be cut and formed into the body of an instrument nobody has seen before.

Coming to the table below the large window, Bart pulls a wooden assembly with ten strings, imitating a portion of the keyboard on a harpsichord, into the sunlight.

"This is what I have come up with," Bart says, pointing to where one of the strings meets the key. "It is an adapting pick. Or will be."

"An adapting pick?"

"Yes. It will be sensitive to how hard you hit the key."

"Okay. Can you show me?"

"I can," Bart says eagerly. He presses the lowest key on the assembly, softly at first, then repeating the motion with growing force. Finishing his demonstration, he looks at Andy, smiling, with pride, but Andy's expression remains flat.

"That is impressive," he says, "but I could barely hear the increase in volume. I could hear your finger hitting the key louder than the sound produced by the string."

Bart quickly dismisses the initial disappointment that pricks his mind, knowing in his heart that Andy is right: his imagination has made it sound louder than it actually is. "I'm glad you said that. I was thinking the same thing."

"It is a strong idea," Andy concedes. "However, I don't think a pick is the answer."

"You don't?"

"No. This is the third time you've tried using a pick like what is on a harpsichord. I think this instrument is going to need something else."

"Okay. I see." Bart pushes the assembly to the back of the table. "It needs something that can forcefully strike the string but also pick it ever-so-softly."

Andy looks at him and says, "You're only just beginning. No stress."

"Seven months feels like quite a while." He had hoped to be further along by now.

Andy chuckled. "When you get as old as me, half a year feels like no time at all."

Bart moves to the pile of lumber. "This is beautiful wood. It will be lavish once I finish sanding and oiling."

"Lavish indeed. So, how is the baby?" Andy changes the subject.

Bart looks at the sun gleaming through the window and then at Andy, taking a slow inhale and exhale. Expressing his heart, he says, "She is perfect in every way."

"That is what you said the last time I asked." Andy laughs. "I am glad for you and your family."

"Thank you. I'll have Adele bring her by one day soon so you can meet her."

"I would love that!" Andy says. "Everyone here would."

Andy is Bart's employer and boss. However, after seven months of working for him, Bart only sees him as an old friend. His wisdom and kindness create an atmosphere of authenticity, where Bart can be himself entirely.

"Well, I must go. It's my and Marsha's day together. I will see you in a few days." Andy shakes Bart's hand. "Oh," he turns to look back at Bart from the doorway, "I want to thank you for showing me the work you created. You never cease to amaze me."

Bart meets Andy's eyes and says, "Thank you."

Andy's gratitude is an encouragement and strikes a well of new ideas in Bart's mind. Before he begins his day by sanding lumber, he pulls out the canvas and easel again. *No more trying to make a pick work. It's time to try something else entirely.*

$$ \clubsuit \, \flat \, \text{🎹} \, \flat \flat \, \text{♫} $$

Arriving home has always been a special part of each day for Bart, especially now that it contains two hearts that have captivated him. Drawing closer to the house, he is filled with a longing for their home in Padua. The thought that his daughter will never know the home he and Adele made together is disappointing. Perhaps he feels this way today because of the letter he sent to Marco recently, stirring up the homesickness he had successfully tucked away. On entering, Adele catches his eye from the kitchen. She wears her flour-coated apron as she moves gracefully throughout, preparing supper. Her flowing blond hair shining like gold from the evening rays of sunlight. He walks to her from the front door where he leaves his boots, kisses her softly, and says, "I love you."

She smiles back at him. "I love you too."

Now that he is in the kitchen with her, he notices Cuori wide awake and watching them with her big green eyes. Adele has her cradle sitting in one of the dining room chairs situated to the left of the kitchen.

"There's my baby girl!" He crouches before her, and when her eyes widen, and she giggles, he lifts her into his arms. "You are the most precious little creature on earth," he murmurs.

"How was your day at the shop?" Adele asks.

"It was alright. A little disappointing," he answers honestly.

"Why disappointing?"

"The adapting pick I told you about?"

"Yeah."

"It is a lost cause."

"Oh, I'm sorry. I know you were excited about it," Adele says with an understanding tone.

"Yes, but I knew it wasn't what we were really wanting. I convinced myself it was better than it was."

"So, what does that mean now?"

"I am essentially starting from scratch. Andy thinks that a pick will never suffice, and I agree," Bart explains as he continues to rock Cuori side to side. Her gaze is fixed on him, and he grins at her.

"Starting from scratch?" Adele sighs. "At least you know now what *doesn't* work."

"That is true. I narrowed down my options of ideas to try," Bart agrees.

"Still excited?"

Bart looks up from Cuori. "Yes! Well, I am trying to be. We've been here over half a year now, and I have only accomplished determining the paths that won't work."

"Hey, you're an inventor." Adele says whimsically. "You know something like this takes time. Besides, Andy has no deadline."

"I know." He smiles at her. "I'm just being impatient, is all."

Adele fills two plates with her homemade pasta and garlic bread. "All good things take time. Look at what you're holding in your arms as evidence."

Bart laughs as he settles Cuori back in her cradle. "You are full of wisdom this evening."

"And?"

"Nothing. I have a wise wife, is all." He smirks.

"You were being sarcastic," she says with mock offense.

"Maybe."

"You're always giving me advice. I thought it was a good time to return the favor," she says, fluttering her eyes.

"And I appreciate it," he laughs.

He grins at her and takes their plates to the table. Adele brings the bread and they settle in chairs across from one another. Bart glances from Adele to the baby and his heart swells at the sight. The three of them occupy the room as a family, he thinks, representing the love and courage required to make it one.

"I met a sweet lady today at the park," Adele says.

"Really? How did you meet?" Bart forks a bite of pasta into his mouth.

"We almost didn't. It was so busy, I almost turned around and came home, but then Anna—that is the lady's name—yelled at me and offered me a place to sit."

"Adele! I am so glad you have made a friend." Bart won't say it, but he's also relieved. He's been concerned that Adele hasn't made friends in Florence as easily as he has. "Where does she live?"

"Only a couple streets down from us. We have plans to meet at the park again tomorrow. She has a baby boy a few weeks older than Cuori."

"That makes it even better, a future playmate for Cuori," he says.

"Yes, I thought of that, too! In my letter to Molly just this morning, I had been complaining about how I have no friends here and how difficult moving has been for me. Florence just hasn't felt like home without her."

"I know it has been hard on you not having Molly, but look, 'it takes time for good things to happen!" He leans over and squeezes her shoulder.

Adele rolls her eyes. "That is true. She is really easy to open up to, and we have a lot of the same childhood experiences. It's hard to build new friendships as an adult, especially with someone who understands you at least a little bit."

"For sure. You're the only person who understands me. I like it that way, though." Bart smiles at her.

"I like it that way too. And you are the one I go to with everything, but as you know, I am someone who needs more than one outlet."

"You have always been the social one in our relationship. You draw people in so naturally."

"Yes! And I have missed being able to do that."

"Well, my dear, I believe Anna is the friend you've been waiting for. Nobody comes into our lives without a reason."

"I agree," Adele says, standing to gather the dishes.

"Don't worry about those. I will put them away," Bart offers. "I'll meet you and Cuori in the bedroom."

"Thank you, my love," she says.

Bart takes his time cleaning and putting away the few dishes they used to serve dinner. He loves to participate in household chores every way he can, more so now that Cuori has arrived, which reduces stress for Adele. Before he heads toward the bedroom, he blows out the three lanterns scattered across the kitchen and dining room table.

Although work was disappointing today, his excitement is still strong. He is finally the father of a perfect daughter, and his wife has found a friend, connecting her to Florence for more than just supporting *his* dreams. An ember of worry remains, though, threatening to grow ablaze. What if he can't pull off the invention of the instrument Andy wants? What if Anna isn't a long-term friend for Adele, their relationship is still premature?

When he arrives at the doorway to their bedroom, he finds Adele and Cuori snuggling in the bed, waiting for him to extinguish the last candle flame and join them. They are all the reminder he needs. *Good things take time. Everything is coming together.*

CHAPTER
Nine

1685 – Adele
A Few Years Later

[Listen to 'Always Only Love You']

A foot jammed into Adele's spine wakes her sharply. She moans internally as she turns to look across the bed, where she finds Bart still fast asleep and Cuori, now wide awake, looking at her.

"I'm sorry, Mama. I didn't mean to kick you," Cuori whispers.

You never do, she thinks.

"It's okay, my love," Adele says, running her hands through her daughter's long blond hair. "Are you ready to start the day?" she asks.

Cuori nods her head, grinning.

They quietly peel themselves from the covers, careful not to wake Bart. Cuori will celebrate her third birthday in a week, but she still wants to sleep with her parents. Adele worries about the

situation, when Cuori is alone, she becomes anxious and so rest-
less she's wakeful all night. While Adele and Bart don't mind her
presence, it is still a blessing, not a nuisance, she is afraid there is
an underlying issue for Cuori's anxiety and what could be so troubling for such a young child is of concern. Their priest has assured
them for now, though, being in the presence of her parents is all
she needs. Until something changes, they shouldn't worry.

The sun is only barely creeping up on the horizon as Adele
and Cuori walk into the front room. Adele lights a candle, and sitting in the rocking chair near the front door, she draws Cuori onto
her lap. They rock back and forth for a time in gentle silence. It is
routine, starting their mornings this way. Cuori taps her finger on
her mother's arm to the beat of her heart, and Adele hears a song
within it. Mother and daughter create rhythm and melody together
in the soft, candlelit room.

"I love you, Mama," Cuori mumbles, and as it always does on
hearing her daughter say this, Adele's heart swells with happiness.

After sitting together for half an hour, she hears Bart yawn
when walking out of the bedroom. The sunlight now spotlights his
entrance and exaggerates his warm, round face and few freckles.
He has already changed into his clothes for the day.

"Papa!" Cuori squeaks.

He leans over and kisses the top of her head. "Good morning,
my angel."

Adele stands to greet him with a kiss. His presence is so pleasing even after many years together.

"What are your plans for the day?" Bart asks, making his way
into the pantry to gather items for his lunch.

"Anna and Luca are coming over, and we are heading to the market and then the park. I'll be working in the garden a few hours before we go."

Bart smiles at her. "Sounds like a perfect day."

"I'm going to play with Luca!" Cuori adds.

"Is that so? Luca is special, isn't he?" Bart asks her.

"Yes." She giggles.

"Is today when you're meeting with the journalists?" Adele pipes in, gazing up at him from where she sits.

"No, that is tomorrow. And I'm really nervous about that still."

"Don't be. They just want to show off the work you've been doing."

"I have not done anything yet. I just have a culmination of failures and this *one* potential idea."

"You give people hope. You're creating something new and beautiful. They only want to talk to you and see what it is," she encourages him, feeling his nervousness herself. *He has never been comfortable with too much attention.*

"Thank you, babe. I'll know today what time we meet tomorrow. I would love it for you two to be there."

"We will be." She smiles at Cuori, who is listening intently, her eyes and ears always so observant. "We are so proud of you, Bart."

"Perfect. I am heading out for the day. Have fun, Cuori!" Bart says, his posture noticeably more relaxed closing the front door behind him.

She turns her attention to Cuori again. "Ready for breakfast and then go outside?"

Cuori nods her head. "Will there be more butterflies?"

"Maybe," she says with magic in her whisper.

In the backyard, the sun is not high enough to have topped the black poplar tree and the garden remains shaded. Adele works her bare toes into the garden soil, liking the feel. Cuori does the same. Barefoot gardening makes for dirty but tough feet, Adele thinks as she retrieves her spade and a small rake from where they rest near the back door.

Dropping to her knees, she begins weeding the row of lavender first. For her the fragrance of the plant remains irresistible. Other rows of vegetables surround her. While the lavender, basil, pepper, and tomatoes are on the right, asparagus, potatoes, and carrots line the left side of the garden.

After a few minutes, Cuori, who is on her knees nearby, begins her mid-morning routine of asking questions.

"Mama. Why do plants grow in dirt?" she asks, dropping a small scoop of soil from her hands.

"Because their roots find food and water in the soil."

"But it is so dirty."

Laughing, she says, "No, it's not!" and tosses a fistful of soil at Cuori's legs.

Cuori giggles. "Hey! You got dirt on me."

"I know. See, it's not dirty. You are completely fine."

"What does nervous mean?"

Adele's lightheartedness falls abruptly away as she turns to focus her gaze on her daughter. "Why do you ask that?"

"Because Papa said he was nervous."

Oh. The syllable rises on a bubble of relief in Adele's brain. "Nervous means you are a teeny bit scared to do something, and you think about it *a lot.*"

"Are you ever nervous?"

"Yeah, sometimes."

"When?"

Adele starts weeding again. "When we go to the market, and there are many people. Sometimes, I'm nervous I will lose you."

Cuori grins. "You could never lose me, Mama."

"I'm so glad," she says.

"I am nervous all the time," Cuori says, her tone carefree.

Adele stops weeding again and shifts from her knees to sit on her bottom. Slightly out of breath from the transition she asks, "Why do you think that?"

"I am always scared something bad will happen."

"Like what?"

"I don't know. When I can't see you or Papa, I get scared."

"I know, sweetie. I know, but you know your papa and I will always be here. Right?" She pulls Cuori's hands to hers.

"Yes."

"Come give me a hug." Adele opens her arms to embrace her daughter, thinking how bright she is for a child not even quite three years old.

Cuori spends the rest of the morning picking a few flowers to encourage a butterfly to chase her, and Adele finishes her weeding. As soon as she puts the rake and spade back in place, she sees Anna and Luca walking along the street.

"What perfect timing," she says when Anna is within earshot, approaching from the side of the house. "We just finished in the garden."

"Lovely!" Anna says, hugging Adele.

Luca runs to meet Cuori, and they immediately start playing tag. Watching them, Adele thinks how Luca is already three and he's two times the size of Cuori. But Cuori has the edge over Luca when it comes to talking. She can form clear and complete sentences, whereas Luca still mumbles and is hard to understand.

Adele looks at Anna. "Let me change clothes and rinse my hands, then we can go." Moments later, she rejoins Anna and the four take off to the market downtown, Cuori and Luca walking in front so Adele and Anna can keep an eye on them.

"How is Bart doing?" Anna asks.

"He is well, he always is. He did admit he was a bit nervous for tomorrow, though."

"What is going on tomorrow?"

"The newspaper journalists are visiting the music hall, and he and Andy are going to talk about the instrument he is inventing."

"I see. Are you going?" Anna asks.

"Yes, Cuori and I both."

"Good. It will help his nervousness for you two to be there and support him during a stressful event," Anna says, but her usual lively tone and her demeanor lack conviction. Almost emotionless.

"For sure. I am excited," Adele says, but glancing sidelong at her friend, she wonders if there is something wrong. "I have only been to the music hall a handful of times, and it is always a special experience."

When Anna doesn't respond Adele tries again. "How is Dario doing?"

"The same, nothing eventful lately. He did get a promotion last Friday, though. I am proud of him."

"That is good news," Adele says cheerfully, and this time when Anna doesn't respond, she hooks her friend's elbow with her hand, and she's on the verge of asking Anna what's troubling her when she hears a man's voice, gritty with anger.

"Don't look at me, you nasty woman. You're worthless, too worthless even to be the prostitute you are."

It comes from up ahead of them, amidst a busy sidewalk intersection close to the market. She and Anna both run and stop their kids. They are close enough now to watch the exchange a few yards before them. The corner of the nearest building casts an eerie shadow. "What in the world?" she barely hears Anna murmur.

Two men in worn work clothes, one tall, one of average height, are verbally harassing a woman who has her back to them. She keeps her head down, covered with a black hood, and ignores them. When she tries to walk away, the taller of the two men jerks her shoulder causing her to stumble and fall to the ground.

Adele feels her pain. *Oh no!*

When the woman brings up her hands, guarding her face, he growls, "You better flinch. You better have some respect, too, the next time I talk to you."

The woman struggles to her feet. "I have no respect for a coward like you," she says boldly.

Adele's hand flies to her mouth when the man kicks her legs from under her, causing her to again fall face-first back to the ground.

"Mama, why is he hurting her?" Cuori asks, her little voice teetering and teary.

"I don't know, precious." Adele cups her hands around Cuori's head, over her ears.

The woman is whimpering, apologetic. "I'm sorry."

"Sorry, doesn't cut it," the shorter of the two men says. "You're going to pay for that comment." And leaning over her, he grabs her arm.

"Why is nobody helping her?" Anna says quietly. "This street is busy, but people are ignoring his abuse."

"Because patrolmen don't care about poor people," she responds.

Something in Adele snaps, and setting Cuori aside, without considering the risk, she walks up to the men. "Leave her alone," she orders them, and within herself she is amazed at the strength in her voice, the sound of her authority.

"Get out of my face, woman," the tall man jeers.

"This doesn't concern you," the shorter of the two says scornfully.

When both men turn back to the woman on the ground, Adele repeats herself loudly above the sound of her pounding heart. Neither one pay her any mind but are intent on jerking the hapless woman to her feet. "I said leave her alone." This time, as Adele speaks, her voice is fiercer, more determined.

"I think we should leave, Hank," the shorter man says, nervously eyeing the gathering crowd. "It's not worth getting in trouble with a citizen over a prostitute."

"Yes, you should leave," Adele asserts. She instinctively knows the shorter man is afraid, and she glares at him.

"No," the one called Hank says. "Now I have two disrespectful women to deal with." He locks Adele's gaze.

"Listen to your friend and walk away," she tells him, refusing to allow him to intimidate her. Too late, she registers the back of Hanks's hand as it slaps her across the face, and she staggers back, collapsing to her knees. Pain consumes her.

"You do not tell me what to do!" Hank yells, towering over her, smirking down at her.

Finding strength and courage she did not know she possessed, Adele scrambles to her feet and before he can react, she kicks him, hard, in his groin.

Hank drops, writhing on the ground, squalling in pain.

Now it is Adele's turn to stand over him. "Get up," she orders. "Leave. Or do you need more convincing?"

The short man helps Hank to his feet, and without a word the two walk away, Hank limping with every step.

Adele's eyes begin to see reality again, and she gently massages the side of her face where Hank's hand hit her. When she turns and takes in her surroundings, she realizes several people have stopped to watch the argument, and many eyes are still on her. Embarrassed, she looks down at the woman lying on the ground, trembling in fear, and says, "Hey, are you alright? They are gone."

When the woman rolls over and picks herself up, Adele immediately recognizes her, and her stomach drops. *The bread-stand bitch.*

CHAPTER
Ten

Adele

*T*heir eyes lock for only a few seconds, but it feels like hours to Adele. This is the woman who made her question her worth and whether it was possible her husband didn't love her. Here, on the ground, is the woman who once attempted to destroy with her words, and who she has just defended.

Before Adele's thoughts solidify, and she says something she might regret, she feels two little arms wrap tightly around her thigh, and looking down, she sees Cuori weeping and clinging to her. Kneeling beside her small daughter, she says. "Look at me."

Cuori meets her gaze, and it breaks Adele's heart. Her face is soaked with tears, and her hair sticks to her cheeks. "Are you okay, Mama?" she whimpers.

"Yes, my love. I am okay." Adele pulls Cuori into her arms, wrapping her tightly against her chest. "Everything is okay. You don't have to worry about anything."

Cuori's breathing is at a sprinter's pace. After a few moments with her head on Adele's chest, she begins using her index finger to tap along with the rhythm of Adele's heartbeat. Forming their song.

She continues to hold fast to Cuori while noticing Anna talking to the woman she defended, unaware Adele already knows the woman. And dislikes her. The crowd dissipated almost as quickly as it formed. Once her heartbeat slows, so do Cuori's taps as they both calm down. Adele straightens, asking Cuori, "Are you okay to finish our walk to the market?" When Cuori nods, Adele squeezes her hand. She finds Anna's gaze. "We are ready if you are," she says.

"Sheila, this is my friend, Adele, and her daughter, Cuori," Anna introduces the woman.

So, Sheila is her name, Adele thinks, and gives her a quick and forced grin.

"Would you like to join us?" Anna asks. "We will be downtown for a little while, then we're going to head back to Adele's house."

What is she doing? Didn't she hear those men's accusations? She is a prostitute! Adele shakes her head subtly, trying to get Anna's attention.

Sheila stutters. Probably just as surprised by Anna's invitation as Adele. Looking at the ground and muttering she says, "I probably should finish my errands."

"Oh, Sheila, just come with us!" Anna says.

Sheila looks at Adele, embarrassed, and something in her expression lets Adele know that Sheila remembers her. "It's okay. I would like it if you would join us, too," she lies. Her kind nature refuses to blatantly insult Sheila by withdrawing Anna's invitation.

"Okay then," Sheila says.

Anna begins walking with Luca by her side. "Well, let's get out of the way and start moving," she says. "Do you two know each other?" she whispers to Adele when she catches up and when Sheila is distracted, answering a question Luca has asked her.

"It's a long story," Adele answers softly.

When they arrive at the park after heading back from the market, Cuori refuses to play with Luca or any other kids. Adele crouches beside her. "You can go play," she reassures. "I'm fine. I promise you don't have to worry about me."

"No. I want to stay beside you," Cuori insists.

Turning to Anna, Adele mouths, "I'm sorry."

Anna waves the apology aside, and when Luca decides he doesn't want to play without Cuori, the five of them walk to Adele's home, where an afternoon snack awaits the women, and a nap awaits the children.

Arriving there, Sheila offers her thanks, but Anna interrupts saying, "Oh no. You're coming inside. Adele makes the best snacks."

Adele bites back a groan. *Anna, let her leave.* The plea rattles through Adele's mind.

Sheila looks at Adele, who forces another smile. "Absolutely. Come on in!"

They troop into the house, and Adele and Anna take Luca and Cuori into the main bedroom to take their usual nap. When Cuori makes no fuss and lets go of Adele's hand, she breathes a sigh of relief. She had worried Cuori might never leave her side. Her little eyes scream exhaustion.

When the women gather in the kitchen, Sheila asks, "Can I rinse my hands?"

Adele points her in the direction of the washroom. "A bowl of clean water is in there, filled this morning."

"Thank you," Sheila says and walks out of the room.

When she is out of view, Anna sets her hands on her hips. "Okay, so how do you know her?"

Adele ignores the question. "Anna. Why did you invite a prostitute into my home?" she asks anxiously.

Seemingly unaware of the worry in Adele's voice, Anna answers, "I don't think she is one."

"And how would you know that?" she presses, confused by Anna's confidence.

"Does she look like one?"

"Well. No. But you heard that man's accusation. Right?"

"I think we should hear her story first. And you're the one who defended her, remember?"

Adele squints her eyes at Anna, slightly annoyed. "That was before I knew who she was."

"Which brings us back to how you've met her already?"

Adele starts pulling items from the pantry and laying them on the counter. "Did I ever tell you about my first experience at the market here in Florence?"

"Yeah, I think," Anna says.

Adele works slowly, unfazed by Anna's urgent need to hear the details. "Remember the bread-stand bitch?"

"Yeah."

Adele tips her glance toward the doorway through which Sheila disappeared, and when Anna's eyes widen, she knows her friend has made the connection.

Anna covers her mouth with her hands, muttering behind them, "Oh no. You're serious?"

"I am," she says, going back to slicing bread.

Anna stifles her laughter, covering it with a coughing fit when Sheila reappears.

"Can I help with anything?" she asks, smiling as if she might join in whatever humor is afoot.

"Yeah, actually. Could you spread the jam?" Adele says.

"Gladly."

Anna manages to regain her composure, and leaning one hand on the countertop she smoothly says, "So, Sheila, Adele told me how you two met."

Adele drops the butter knife and glares at Anna, throwing invisible arrows of anger at her.

Sheila's face grows bright red.

Anna smirks into the pot she's stirring, taking a seat on a stool across the counter from them.

Adele wants to kill them both.

Silence fills the kitchen as Adele resumes spreading butter on the bread she has sliced and then hands it, wordlessly, to Sheila to spread the jam.

It's Anna who speaks finally, asking Sheila, "Are you okay?" in her sweet voice.

Looking covertly at Sheila, Adele notices the woman wiping a tear from her eye.

Sheila puts the spoon down and says, "No." She pauses.

Feeling her glance, Adele keeps her focus on the bread. It is so awkward, she thinks. What is she going to say?

"I'm so sorry, Adele, for what I said that day."

An apology isn't what Adele expected to hear. In any case, she won't accept it so easily. "Really?" she asks tartly. "You seemed quite confident in your words." *Just say something like you did then. I'll chew you up and spit you out. This is my home.* The thoughts crease Adele's brain.

"I know. And I am sorry. I judged you without even knowing your name and treated you unkindly."

Anna sits across from where Adele and Sheila stand, saying nothing, only watching and listening. When she tries to reach for a slice of bread with jam and butter, Adele slaps her hand. "Not yet," she hisses. Anna pulls her hand back and holds it against her chest as if she were bitten by a snake.

"But why were you so rude? You made me question myself and my marriage." Adele feels a resurgence of her anger from three years ago, and she can't keep herself from unleashing it. The same heat is rising inside her just like it did then. Thankfully, her hands are busy with the bread. Otherwise, she might not be able to control her urge to punch the bitch.

"I was rude because I was jealous. You were happy and expecting. I saw potential fragility in your story and wanted to expose it to make you feel bad. Make you feel as badly as I did," Sheila admits, honest emotion making her stutter.

"Oh," Adele says, having no idea how to respond. To her relief, Sheila continues.

"My husband and I were married when I was fourteen. I was never able to have his baby, so eventually he left me. A divorced woman is worthless, and nothing has changed. Now I'm almost fifty and..." She trails off and starts to cry. "And now I have sold my body to one of the lowest men in Italy just to have enough money to survive. I'm a worthless prostitute."

"Sheila. You are not worthless," Anna consoles.

"Of course I am. Look at what happened today. If it weren't for Adele, that man might have killed me, and nobody would care."

"I care," Anna says.

"And obviously, I do, too," Adele says. She doesn't like the woman any better, she thinks, but neither did she deserve to feel worthless. "Do you still... You know?

Sheila shakes her head. "No, just that man a few weeks ago. I became so desperate for money. But still I sold myself."

Anna stands up and walks around the counter and hugs Sheila. Adele wraps her arms around her, too. Neither of them says anything as Sheila cries quietly, shoulders shaking.

Somehow, as Adele embraces the woman, she feels a warmth of mercy and grace begin to fill her. It's not that she has forgotten what Sheila said or how it made her feel, but those cruel words and the way she was affected by them seem smaller to her. Clearly what caused Sheila to lash out in that manner was her own hidden pain and suffering.

"Thank you," Sheila whispers, when at last Adele and Anna let her go.

"Hey. You are a friend now. We have your back," Anna says.

"Absolutely. We are here for you," Adele adds, meaning what she says now.

"You literally cut a man down to his knees and made him cry." When Sheila chuckles, Adele and Anna laugh, too.

"Yeah, where did that come from?" Anna asks, taking her plate of bread and jam Adele finally allows her.

Adele and Sheila both take a plate as well, and the three of them walk into the living area, forming a small circle with the seats chosen.

"I don't know, honestly. When I watched how he was treating you, my mind went blank, and all I knew to do was help however I could."

"It was incredible. You took him by such surprise and stood your ground better than he did." Anna beams.

"I can't describe how good it felt to have someone defend me. I'm so sorry he slapped you," Sheila says.

"It's fine. Doesn't even hurt anymore."

"That's good, but it is bruising," Anna says.

Touching her cheek, she thinks of Bart's interview tomorrow and worries it will show. "It will heal fast, hopefully," she says. "I am surprised I did it, though. I'm actually a timid person."

"Well, you didn't seem timid at all. You were a bold and brave woman!" Anna shouts quietly. Careful to not wake the napping children.

"And that is putting it lightly," Sheila says, and their laughter consumes the room.

The three women finish the snack they prepared, and Adele and Anna learn a few more pieces of Sheila's story, their hearts filling with empathy for their new friend.

Later, they're talking quietly when Luca appears, rubbing his eyes. He crawls into his mama's lap.

"Ready to go home?" she asks him.

He nods and leans on her shoulder. She kisses the top of his head, then stands and says, "Ladies, thank you for a lovely afternoon. It's time for us to go."

"I must go, too," Sheila says.

"Bye, Luca," Adele says as they all walk to the door.

"Bye, Aunt Adele."

Adele feels a rush of love mixed with delight at being called an aunt. "He has stolen my heart," she says, looking at Anna.

Anna smiles. "He has the best aunt. Love you."

"Thank you for your kindness this afternoon. I've enjoyed myself very much," Sheila says.

"We appreciate you too, Sheila. Come by anytime. Anna and I meet every Monday, Wednesday, and Friday. Come by one day or all of them," Adele says. As she gives a final wave and closes the door, she realizes she means it, that she honestly does hope to see Sheila become a close friend. It has been such an interesting day, she thinks, returning to her chair. She notices the quiet of the house, but where she usually finds it exhausting, now it is relaxing to be left alone with her thoughts.

"Hi, Mama." Cuori's quiet voice breaks the silence.

"Hi, baby." Adele holds out her arms to Cuori, who is standing in the bedroom doorway, and when she comes running, Adele scoops her up.

"Mama?" Cuori lifts her head from Adele's chest.

"Yes, Cuori?"

"I like Sheila."

"You do? Why is that?"

"She is nice."

"I think so too. But you didn't even talk to her?" she questions.

"I watched her and listened to her," Cuori says.

"You did? What seemed the nicest about her then?"

"She told you she was sorry."

Adele's chest tightens. How much had she heard?

"Mama, did she say something mean to you?" Cuori asks, her consuming green eyes beaming up at Adele.

She struggles to find the words to speak. "Um, she did say some mean things to me a long time ago, but I forgave her."

"What does 'forgave' mean?"

"It means to let go of anger and hate for someone because of what they said or did," Adele explains, reminding herself even as she teaches her daughter.

"Do you forgave me?" Cuori asks, lowering her head back to Adele's chest.

"Forgive you for what?"

"When you get mad at me for not listening sometimes."

"Cuori, listen closely."

Cuori meets Adele's gaze. "I am never angry with you. I am never disappointed in you. I will always only love you with all my heart."

"Okay."

"Never forget it."

"I won't, Mama."

Cuori falls silent, and Adele rocks gently back and forth, feeling Cuori grow heavy with sleep. Her nap time was apparently used to listen to the women's conversation, not to rest.

Reflecting on all that has happened today, Adele thinks how harshly she judged Sheila, first labeling her the bread-stand bitch. But today, what she saw in Sheila was treasure, hidden gold. The reality is she should never have judged Sheila at all, only listened. Instead, she took offense.

CHAPTER
Eleven

Bart

*N*ervous sweat threatens to soak Bart's shirt, undermining his effort to maintain a confident composure. The journalists from Florence's weekly newspaper are scheduled to arrive any moment, and Bart and Andy are waiting in his shop. He would be much calmer if Adele could be here too, like they had initially planned. But she was too embarrassed to be seen in public because of the bruise on her face caused by the fall from yesterday she had told him about.

By contrast, Andy appears cool and unflustered. Bart can't help but envy his composure, always comfortable and never on edge. Bart thinks how he would love to know Andy's secret. The interview today is their one chance to prove they are building a new instrument of significance. If Bart fails to impress them, the entire city of Florence will question his abilities and purpose for being at the music hall. Andy's status as a renowned composer could even be at risk since he is the one who hired him. People in Florence are quick to praise but even quicker to criticize.

"How are you just standing there?" Bart can't help asking. "Aren't you nervous too?"

Andy huffs and smiles at him. "Of course I'm nervous, but I breathe through it. You pace and sweat through it," he says arms crossed.

"Well, you don't look nervous," Bart says.

"When your career requires you to be in the public eye on a regular basis, you eventually get used to it."

"Yeah, you're a musician, so you know how to manage an interview like this. I'm a builder, and God didn't make someone with craftsmanship *and* people skills. I get nervous when I have to talk to anyone, much more when it involves important people."

Andy's laughter fills the room, but Bart isn't joking. He continues his pacing until Andy walks up to him and places both hands on his shoulders. "Son," he begins, with a fatherly tone, "you will be fine. I know you're anxious, but you know what you're talking about. What you've invented so far is astounding, and they will undoubtedly be impressed. Just take deep breaths and trust what you know. I'll be here the whole time, too."

Bart nods. "Okay. I can do this."

Just as Andy steps back, Antonio comes into the shop with four other men.

"Good morning, Scipione!" Andy greets the shortest and oldest man in the group. A round of introductions follows and before they finish, Bart notices Antonio slip away. Possibly Antonio is uncomfortable, too, in such situations, Bart thinks.

"Where should we begin?" Andy asks.

Scipione—the lead journalist—pulls out a wax tablet with a single page left on it. "If you want to show us the instrument being built, we will have a few questions to ask along the way."

"Perfect," Bart says. "Will you come this way?" He leads them to the far wall where a table stretches from one side of the room to the other under the largest window in the shop. As they pass by the frame Bart has built for his invention, it catches the attention of two of the journalists, Matteo and Aldo. He can hear them murmuring about it, and his pulse taps.

Bart slides a large frame to his side on the table. It has about twenty long strings stretched across it.

"What is this?" Scipione asks.

"This is the skeleton of my invention. You'll notice the strings are similar to a harpsichord, but the picking mechanism is missing."

"I see that," Scipione says, looking intrigued. "How does it work?"

"I'm happy to demonstrate," Bart says, and taking a small pick out of his pocket he uses it to flick one of the strings. The room immediately fills with a soft sound. "The picking mechanism works just like my hand would if I were to flick the string with my fingers. It gets the job done but lacks the ability to vibrate the whole string and therefore doesn't produce a fully resounding tone."

Bart turns and picking up a wooden hammer with felt wrapped around the hammer's head, holding it aloft, he says, "But if I use this there is a difference. Listen." He strikes the same string with the padded hammer, and the sound explodes into the room. Intense vibrations echo with loud and rich tones from the walls, the floor, the ceiling. The eyes of all four journalists open wide, and Scipione's mouth drops slightly. Bart lets the sound slowly fade instead of using his hand to end the note.

"The hammer, when used to strike the string, vibrates the entire length of it, releasing a far greater level of sound and quality of tone," he explains.

"I didn't know a stringed instrument could sound like that!" Gianni, the youngest-looking journalist, says.

"This instrument will not be considered a stringed instrument but percussion because of the use of a hammer that strikes the string," Andy says.

Bart is pleased to see that the four journalists are writing as fast as possible.

Looking up at Bart from his notepad, Scipione asks, "Will it still have a keyboard?"

"Yes," Bart answers proudly. "I have much work still to do, but I plan for each key to be attached to a hammer."

"Wow," Scipione says. "This is remarkable!"

"I could feel the vibrations in my chest. Even just hearing one note struck like that, I can imagine the melodies played would be immensely powerful," Matteo says.

Bart feels his heart become calmer, and he is overcome with the warmth of happiness. It is all going so much better than he could have hoped.

"How long did it take for you to come up with the hammer idea?" Scipione asks.

Bart looks to Andy, and when he nods, Bart continues. "About two years. I was inspired by the hammered dulcimer. Although the end result is going to be nothing like a dulcimer."

Scipione's eyes widen. "Two years! I hope it doesn't take that long to finish it," he says with an excited laugh.

Bart laughs, too. "You and me both. I don't expect it to, not once I figure out exactly how the hammers will be attached to the keys."

Now the whole group laughs, all except Andy, Bart notices. He characteristically maintains his wise and calm composure.

"Andy, you mentioned you hired Bart specifically for building this instrument. Was it your idea?" Scipione asks.

"No," Andy answers at once. "Everything here is Bart's idea, the result of his creativity, followed by trial and error."

"What prompted you to hire *him* for this task, though?" Scipione presses.

"I felt the instruments available today are not capable of fulfilling my vision. My compositions have evolved over time and continue to do so, but now they require a depth and emotion the harpsichord cannot offer. I sought out Bart for his craftsmanship, having composed many arrangements on harpsichords he built, I knew he was the one for the job."

"So, this will be like a harpsichord?"

Andy glances at Bart, leaning now against the table and lets him answer. "It will be similar to a harpsichord, as you can see by the frame." He points behind them to the frame of the instrument-in-progress in the center of the room. "The keyboard on this instrument, however, as I said, it will be nothing the same as a harpsichord internally. It will not be a stringed instrument but percussion."

Watching the journalists, Bart sees they continue to take down every word he says.

"I think we have all we need," Scipione says, glancing at the others beside him. "Thank you for the invite. What you are doing here is amazing. We can't wait to let the public know."

"We appreciate your time," Andy says. "And yes, this will be exciting news for Florence."

Bart and Andy follow the journalists to the door, discussing other projects the Florentine Court is involved in, such as shows at the music hall and their constant search for the most talented musicians in Italy.

"Oh," Scipione says, stopping suddenly at the threshold, and turning, "I almost forgot. What will the instrument be called?"

"The pianoforte," Bart and Andy reply in perfect unison, giving Scipione and his cohorts the name they have come up with, and the two exchange a joyful glance, as Bart repeats it, "The instrument will be called the pianoforte."

CHAPTER
Twelve

1682 – Bart
Later the same day

*B*art's walk home each evening never fails to end in a long pause just before entering his house to admire the glow of the setting sun as it lights up his home and trees in the backyard. As beautiful as it is, Bart can't help but be reminded of Padua, his *real* home. Thinking of Padua reminds him of Marco, whom he hasn't written to since Cuori's second birthday. Almost a year ago. *I'll write to him in the morning*, he thinks as he approaches the walkway leading to the porch. The purple and yellow wildflowers Adele planted in the front flower beds now droop over some of the rock pathway and leave small dustings of pollen on his dark pants.

He quickly ascends a few steps and enters the house. Before the door closes behind him, the sound of little footsteps announces Cuori as she bursts into view.

"Papa!" she screams on catching sight of him, and she runs to him, open armed, trusting Bart to catch her.

"My darling Cuori!" he says, swinging her up and lifting her into the air.

"I missed you today," she says seriously.

"I missed you even more."

"I love you, Papa," she says, laying her head against his chest.

"I love you too," he whispers and kisses the top of her head.

He's settling into his chair when Adele walks into the room, but his joy on seeing her and his smile flattens instantly as he registers the worsening injury to her face that appears more swollen than it did yesterday. "Baby, your face."

Adele rolls her eyes. "I love you too."

"Sorry." He smirks. "I love you. But the bruising is so much darker and the swelling has worsened. It looks as if it hurts. Does it?"

"Yes, but nothing I can't stand." She sits down in a chair beside him.

"I'm so sorry, Adele. I wish I could have caught your fall." He gently touches her cheek.

"You and me both," she says, chuckling.

Cuori mumbles something inaudible, and Adele jerks upright. "Not now, Cuori," she says.

"What did you say, Cuori?" Bart asks his daughter.

"I'm sure it was nothing, right, Cuori?" Adele sounds anxious.

Bart looks curiously at her, taking in her reddened face, her breath that seems to come in shortened gasps. "Adele—" he begins, but Cuori, who is leaning on his knee, interrupts him.

"I said, Mama's face is so bad because the mean man hit her so hard."

Bart sits silently for a short moment, then says, "Cuori, Mama fell at the playground, remember?"

Adele stands up. "Honey," she says extending her hand to Cuori, "let's go to your room. I need to talk to your papa alone for a minute."

"I don't want to," Cuori whines.

Bart stares at Adele. "Is it true? Someone hit you?"

"Cuori, you need to go to your room, now." Adele takes a step toward their daughter.

Bart's heart has begun to pound. "Adele, what happened?" He is leaning forward now, and looking at Cuori, he reiterates her mother's demand. "Go to your room, darling, like your mother said."

He watches his daughter finally obey. She slides off his knee and walks in the direction of her room.

"Adele?" Bart says softly when Cuori is out of sight.

She sighs, then sitting down again, she leans forward with her elbows on her knees and covers her face with her hands.

"Are you going to say anything?" Bart feels a pang of annoyance mixed with hurt. He can't believe she lied.

"Yes, Bart, someone—a man—did hit me yesterday."

He stares at his wife in disbelief even as he fills with anger at the unknown assailant and at Adele for not telling him the truth. As calmly as he can manage, he asks, "Who was the man? How did this happen?"

"Anna and I were walking to the market," Adele begins in a voice that wavers over tears. "We came upon two men who were arguing with a woman, saying despicable things. They pushed her to the ground, Bart—" Breaking off, Adele turns to him, and he can see remembered fear and outrage in her eyes.

"Go on," Bart says in a low voice. "What sort of men were they? Did you know the woman?"

Adele is crying now, and he watches as she makes a visible effort to stop. Regaining a bit of her composure, she says, "The men were brutes. The woman was—she was—"

"What, Adele? What was she?" But Bart feels he already knows what she is about to say and his stomach knots.

"The men said she was a—a prostitute." Adele's voice skids over the word. She doesn't look at Bart but at her tear-speckled hands twisting in her lap.

"So, you confronted men who were verbally abusing a prostitute on the street?"

Adele nods.

"That doesn't sound like you. Why didn't you turn around and walk away? You should never be anywhere near people like that. They can hurt you. They did hurt you!" Bart's throat constricts, and he feels his own tears sear his eyes. He feels the heat of his face and imagines it matches Adele's. "Our daughter was there, what if..." Bart can't finish.

"I know!" Adele cries out. "I know. I just felt in my heart suddenly that I needed to protect the woman."

"Did you feel it in your heart to lie to me about it?" He locks her gaze.

"No," she whispers.

Bart's tears dry in the wave of fury that engulfs him—at Adele. It is a feeling he has never had toward her, and he is on his feet before he can think, yelling at her before he can reconsider. "You can only whisper now, but before you could confidently lie and tell me you fell at the park."

"I'm sorry, Bart," she says softly still.

"Speak up. I can't hear you!" he shouts, towering over her, and slaps his hand against the small table beside his chair.

Adele flinches. "I'm sorry." Her voice rises, matching his in intensity.

"I can't believe this, Adele. You put your life and our daughter's life in danger for what? A prostitute?"

"I know it sounds crazy, but I also know it was the right thing to do."

"Then why did you *lie*? I thought we would *never* lie to each other."

"I'm so sorry. I was worried you would be upset and didn't need to be when your interview was today."

"Don't blame this on me."

"I'm not!" she yells again. "I was scared and assumed it would be easier to lie for now and deal with the truth later."

Bart sits down again and reaches for her hand, and she allows it. "Adele," he says more gently, "why would you be scared to tell me what really happened?"

She wipes her tears. "It's not that complicated. I wasn't scared of *you*, but the situation. I guess I needed time to figure out how to tell you. But I am so sorry for lying to you."

Bart draws in his breath. Letting himself relax. Already regretting the way he has just behaved. "I'm sorry for yelling at you. I shouldn't have, but I am still angry with you and need some time to calm down."

"Okay," Adele says. "I'll start dinner."

"I'm going to check on Cuori." Getting up, he crosses the room, thinking how his little girl is probably scared to death from all the yelling, and a sand of guilt rises in his mind.

Arriving at her bedroom doorway, he looks into the room but doesn't see her. "Cuori?" he says to the empty room.

No response.

He walks back down the hall to the kitchen, expecting to find her there with her mother, but she isn't there either. Without saying anything to Adele, he checks their bedroom and the washroom. The last two rooms in the house. There's no sign of her. The slow drum of panic bangs against his chest. Backtracking to the kitchen, he says to Adele, "I can't find Cuori."

Looking up from where she is peeling an onion, she says, "She might have been scared and hid under our sheets."

"I looked. She's not there."

"Really? Let me see." Deserting the kitchen, Adele conducts her own search, while Bart waits in the kitchen, trying to keep himself calm.

"Cuori?" Adele is calling their daughter's name over and over. Adele will find her, Bart thinks.

But when his wife comes back into the kitchen, her face is troubled. "She isn't here."

"I'll look in the front yard, and you check the back," Bart says.

Adele agrees and they run out of opposite doors, but their outdoor search is no more productive than their indoor search.

Meeting again at the front of the house, Bart says breathlessly, his fear stealing his oxygen, "You stay here in case she comes back. I'll ask the neighbors if they have seen her."

"Okay, but hurry," Adele says, and Bart can tell from the way she is shaking, and how pale she is that she's on the verge of becoming hysterical.

As Bart crosses their front yard, his walk turns into a sprint. *My little miracle. Where are you?*

He knocks harshly on their neighbor's door; Albert is the man's name, and he lives alone. "What do you think you're doing beating on my door like that?" Albert asks, angrily opening the door and greeting him.

"Have you seen Cuori this evening?" He tries to keep from sounding panicked.

"Who is Cuori?"

"My daughter," he says, annoyed now. Albert knows very well who she is.

"Oh. I didn't know what her name was. I haven't seen her." His tone softens with sympathy.

"Thank you," Bart says hurriedly as he runs toward the next house in the neighborhood. Albert remains at his doorway. Instead of returning inside, he steps onto his patio and sits facing the street.

House after house, neighbor after neighbor on his side of the street gives him the same answer, that they haven't seen her. He then crosses the street, although he's unsure why as they never go in that direction as it is a dead end. He sees Adele, still sitting on the front steps of their home as he nears their house.

"Nothing?" she asks, trembling.

"No," Bart tells her. Bending over and resting his hands on his knees, he takes a moment to catch his breath, then gesturing, he says, "I'll try those houses now."

Soon, a pink-hued cheek and a hazel-green eye catch his attention. "Cuori!" he shouts, stopping in his tracks.

She steps out from behind a massively trunked maple tree in their neighbor's yard. Bart can see her face is downcast, her shoulders hunched, and her hands squeezed together. He approaches her quicker than lightning but as gently as a summer breeze, and kneeling in front of her, he cups her face in his hands. "Cuori, are you okay?"

She nods, not looking at him.

Looking past her, he examines the tree, noting that it is only half alive. A portion of the trunk has been removed by decay, creating a hollow area big enough that it completely concealed Cuori inside it. Scooping his small daughter into his arms, he spins with her in a joyful and relieved circle. *Thank you, God. My little girl is safe. I have her, and she is safe.* His prayer of gratitude whispers through his mind.

He carries Cuori home, and on seeing them, Adele stands. She remains at the top of the stairs almost as if she is frozen by shock that has now turned to profound relief. Bart himself is still feeling it, the stiffness of fear in his muscles, the deep thud of his heart.

"I'm sorry, Papa," Cuori says softly in his ear.

"Shhh, we will talk later. I'm so happy I found you." Bart cuddles her close.

When he approaches the steps heading into the house, he locks eyes with Adele, and says, "We found her, and she is safe!"

Adele covers her mouth with her hands, and tears roll down her cheeks.

In a joyful expression of finding his daughter safe and sound, he leaps up the steps toward Adele—eyes still locked with hers—but instead of landing solidly, his foot catches on the edge of the bottom step, pulling him to his knees with Cuori in his arms. Trying to correct his fall, he lunges forward with his torso and left leg, which only speeds up his descent toward the jagged steps beneath him. He collapses harshly onto the middle of the small flight of steps, protecting Cuori's head with his hands, but his knee crushes onto her left leg. A crunching sound fills his ears above the moan coming from his chest.

"Bart!" Adele screams.

Groaning, he squirms, trying to get a look at Cuori, terrified she is hurt. Adele bends over both of them, and Bart sees her fear. "Careful," he murmurs.

"Papa?" Cuori's voice breaks on a sob. "It hurts."

"Be still, little one, if you can," he says. "Mama will get you."

"Can you lift yourself a bit?" Adele asks, anxiously. "I think I can get to her then."

Gritting his teeth against the pain, he does manage to maneuver himself, and he feels Adele slide Cuori from beneath him, but he's not prepared for the agonized scream that erupts from his daughter as she's lifted. It explodes into the air, shattering his heart.

"My leg!" she cries out.

CHAPTER
Thirteen

1690 – Cuori
Five Years Later

*T*he sound of children laughing dances to her ears as she and her mama arrive at the park. Cuori doesn't particularly enjoy the park itself but rather the walk to it. She has grown into a strong and healthy eight-year-old girl with a maturity level vastly exceeding any other her age. The trip from their home to the park takes less than ten minutes, and the cool November air stirs around them.

"Why couldn't Anna and Luca come with us today?" Cuori asks.

"I'm not sure. Anna didn't walk Luca to school this morning like usual. Was Luca in class?"

"No."

"He must have been sick today. His mother mentioned he has had a bad cough lately."

"Okay."

"You still want to go to the park, right?"

"Yeah!" Cuori answers excitedly, although for a different reason.

"Good, you two seem to play with a lot of different kids than each other anyway," Adele says.

"Yeah, because he is crazier than I am."

"Oh, so you're too serious to play with him?" Adele chuckles.

"Exactly," Cuori affirms with a straight face.

When they step onto the playground, Cuori takes her mother's hand and says, "Want to see where I like to play?"

"Of course!"

She leads her past the swings and up a small hill toward an enormous hedge that separates the park from the street.

"You'll have to crawl a little bit."

"Crawl? Inside the bushes?"

"Yes, Mama." Cuori sighs dramatically.

"Okay then." Adele obeys, looking around to ensure nobody sees her about to crawl into the massive row of shrubbery.

Cuori scoots easily into an open area in between the branches and leaves and patiently waits for her mother to join her, shuffling her way in beside her.

"So, this is where you go when we are in the park?"

She nods. "Look." She uses both hands to part a section of branches to reveal a clear view of the park.

"Wow. You can see everything easily from this angle."

"Yep," she says proudly. "It's how I always know when it is time to go. I can see when you stand up to leave."

"Sly, aren't you, missy?"

Cuori chuckles to herself. *You have no idea, Mama.*

"Why do you like it in here, though? Do other children come in and play? Or talk?"

"Sometimes, but mostly it's just me."

"What do you do?"

"I like to watch people," she answers.

"Hmm." Adele seems to contemplate. "Why? Are people funny to you?"

"Sometimes, but usually they are interesting."

"Interesting, how?" Adele asks.

"You ask a lot of questions, Mama." Cuori smirks.

"Ugh. You made me crawl inside a bush; I should be allowed to ask as many questions as I want to!" Adele says, making them both laugh.

"I like watching how people act around each other and predicting what they will do."

"Do you ever guess right?"

"Always."

"You're a confident girl today."

Cuori shrugs. "I'm just good at knowing things, I guess."

"Yes, you are. You are so much like your father."

You tell me that all the time, she thinks.

Although she might have a personality a lot like her papa, everyone tells her that she looks just like her mama. They do share blond hair, but hers is already showing signs of turning auburn as she grows older.

"I look like you, though."

"Thank goodness. Imagine if you had a beard." Adele smiles.

Cuori erupts into laughter, causing a few kids playing in the park to look in their direction. "Yes, Mama, you are so pretty. I hope I always look like you." She watches her mama's face almost melt with sentiment.

"I need to go," Adele says after clearing her throat. "I can't be cramped up in here much more. I can go sit on a bench if you want to stay longer," she offers.

"No. I'm ready to go, too."

The walk home is faster than before, a slight competition between them. An after-school ritual when it is just the two of them. "You can only fast-walk, no running!" Adele reminds Cuori as she walks speedily behind her daughter.

"I'll still beat you!" Cuori shouts, reducing her stride from a run to a walk at her mother's request.

"What are you ladies up to?" their neighbor, Albert, asks with a friendly smile, taking a break from pruning his shrubbery.

"We are racing!" Cuori says, focused on touching the lawn before her mother does.

Adele smiles and rolls her eyes at him. "She is a competitive one."

"Looks fun. Have a good evening," he says.

"Thank you, Albert," Adele says, nearly cut off by Cuori's victory shout.

Adele walks into their home first, holding the door open. Cuori follows behind her and heads immediately to her room. She still sleeps with her parents but puts her own room to good use throughout the day.

The first object to catch her eye when she walks into her room is the pale white-colored cast, the same one used to protect her broken leg while it healed when she was three years old. It hangs on her wall as if it were a trophy. Although it was a somewhat tragic event—or so she is told—seeing the cast every time she is in her room reminds her of the way her parents would carry her around everywhere she went. Even from one side of a room to the other. The memory makes her chuckle.

She reaches for a novel, sitting on a tiny, purple bookshelf under the window, and then lies on her bed, turning the pages to the spot she left waiting for her return since this morning. Having books to read in her own home is a privilege. One her father's boss, Andy, makes possible.

One would hardly associate the room with a child except for the linen stuffed animals lined up on her bed. Otherwise, books, newspapers, and art supplies encompass the room. It is nothing short of inspiring. Works of art she created herself hang on the walls. Portraits of people who don't exist outside her mind. Young energy mixed with ages of wisdom fills the atmosphere of the room. The time she spends in here is her only time of privacy, where her true identity and desires are unmasked, and she can do what she loves. Read and daydream.

After almost an hour of reading, she closes the novel, rises from her bed, and walks the short distance to her canvas and easel in the opposite corner of her room. She looks intently at her drawing thus far, her attempt to recreate a scene from the story she is reading. A meadow of wildflowers so detailed and intricate it would overwhelm even the most experienced artists. She takes it daily, only a few flowers at a time.

This will be the most beautiful painting in the world when I am done, she thinks as she sits on her stool, leans over gently, and keenly focuses on each movement of her hand. *And I will give it to Roald!*

Just as the evening sun begins to change the color of her room, she hears the sound of the front door closing and her father's voice echoing softly through the house. *Papa is home!*

Cuori puts her pencil on the art table and bursts out from her room to greet her papa. Tradition remains strong in the Cristofori household. Warm welcomes are abundant and dramatic.

"Cuori!" Bart says as she runs toward him. He still picks her up in his arms, though, she can tell by the strain in his voice when lifting her up that the time he can no longer do so is drawing near.

"I missed you!" she exclaims. She loves her mama, and her time with her. But she feels closer to her papa. He understands her better.

"I missed you too," Bart says, quickly setting her back to her feet.

"Ready to eat?" Adele asks with her back toward them, focused on draining the water off the pasta.

"Absolutely," Bart says, kissing the back of her warm neck.

Watching them, Cuori notices how her mama's eyes light up when her father touches her.

Cuori helps bring the meal to the dinner table, and once they've all settled in their places her father asks his usual question. "How was school today?"

"Boring as always." She gives her usual answer through a mouthful of bread.

"One of these days, you will tell me how much you enjoyed school," he says, smiling at her.

"Unlikely," she replies, focused on the food in front of her. "They teach nothing interesting."

"You still don't find math interesting?"

Her father shoots her a curious look, one that prompts her to respond by sticking out her tongue and wrinkle her nose in disgust. She's gratified when her parents laugh.

"Did you make any new friends today? The city is growing quite quickly, you must meet new children every day?"

"Nope," Cuori answers without looking at her father.

"Do you even talk to other kids?"

"Nope."

"I figured. How come?" he asks, his tone unsurprised.

She becomes slightly annoyed at her father's drilling questions. *We've already been through this before, Papa,* she thinks. "They are only interested in childish things. Which are boring to me." She answers him with emphasis on the O in boring.

"They are *kids*, Cuori," her mother says, as if she needed reminding.

"Yeah. And they don't have much substance."

"You're a kid too, remember? And where did you learn that word? Are you becoming a young Aristotle?" Adele chuckles.

"I know, but I don't like talking to other kids much. Is that bad?" she asks. "And I learned it in the book Papa brought me."

"Not at all, but you shouldn't call them boring or say they don't have substance. It's rude," Adele says in a motherly way. "Knowing many words is good but using them to be kind is far more important."

"Got it," she says.

"You are the smartest kid in Italy!" Her father beams. "Other kids look up to you, I'm sure, so always remember to be nice."

"Oh, I am. I'm nice all the time."

"I know you are, and your mother and I are so proud of you."

"Thanks, Papa! What did you do at the shop today?" she asks, always infatuated with his work.

Bart sighs. "Well, I tested my hammer mechanism."

She watches her mother look at him with beaming eyes. "And did it work?"

Bart looks down at the table. "No, but why would it?" he asks, an edge of sarcasm in his voice. "I mean, five years of testing an idea isn't enough. What kind of idiot keeps trying for this long?"

"Not an idiot, Bart. A dedicated man, inventing something the world has only dared to dream of," Adele says.

Cuori watches silently as her father becomes emotional, seemingly angry but also on the verge of tears. She is used to him admitting his struggle in building the pianoforte, but tonight he seems especially discouraged.

Bart looks up at Adele. "I'm beginning to understand why it's only been a dream."

"Really? You've waited until now to admit you think it's impossible? After you have dedicated almost nine years to it?" Adele asks.

Cuori watches her father's disappointed eyes look into her mother's. "I'm just tired of working so hard on something that has yet to become anything of value. I feel like I am wasting my time."

"Bart, the most valuable things in life sometimes take the longest to become a reality," Adele says, glancing at Cuori. Her father smiles as he gazes at her too.

The look that passes between her parents is laden with meaning, but Cuori is bewildered by it. She feels as though she said something they both were impressed with. She wants to ask but before she can her father starts speaking.

"I could be dedicating myself to something else that has more of an impact *now*," he continues, dropping his momentary smile.

"Maybe your impact on the world doesn't come through words or your invention, but through feeling," Adele says.

"What do you mean?" he asks.

Cuori is curious what her mother means too. She leans forward, watching every movement of her parents' eyes and hand gestures.

"Isn't the pianoforte supposed to be the most expressive instrument? More powerful and capable than any other?" Adele asks.

"Yeah. That is the goal, at least," he answers.

"Then your impact will be revealed in how the music played on the pianoforte makes people *feel*, not through the advent of the instrument itself. Shift your focus." Adele speaks with wisdom and enthusiasm.

Bart sits with Adele's words for a moment, then relaxes back into his chair.

Cuori remains leaning forward, ready to give her input now. "Papa," she says.

"Yes, Cuori." Bart moves his focus to her.

"Your time isn't wasted. I know you will find a way to invent the pianoforte exactly how it's supposed to be."

"Thank you, darling. I needed to hear that," he says, and looks at Adele. "What you said, too." Then he pulls her into his arms for a hug from his seat at the end of the table where Cuori and Adele sit on opposite sides of him. Cuori joins them in their tight squeeze, a family held together by a love that grows each and every day.

When nighttime arrives, just as Adele and Bart lie in bed, Cuori comes in with her book. She shuffles her way between both parents until she finds a comfortable position with her head on her mother's chest. She listens for her heartbeat, then taps along to it on her mama's arm. "Tu tump. Tu tump. Tu tump," she whispers. Her own heartbeat matches its rhythm.

The pulsing sounds slowly lull her to rest only moments after her father blows out the candle. Cradled in her parents' arms, a book held close, the sound of her mother's beating heart and father's steady breathing is the perfect way to end a day and fall asleep.

CHAPTER
fourteen

Cuori

*C*uori is jolted awake as her shoulder—previously supported by her dad—falls flat against the bed when he climbs out to start his day. She is used to waking up at the same time he does and spending a bit of the morning with him before he leaves for work each day.

She lies in bed next to her still slumbering mother until Bart comes out of the washroom, having rinsed his face and dressed in his dusty woodworking clothes. She slides out of bed, quietly, and meets him in the living room.

"Good morning, Papa," she whispers, rubbing both her eyes.

"Good morning, darling. Did you sleep well?"

"Yes."

Bart smiles at her and kisses the top of her head. Sitting down, he draws her onto his lap, a ritual which she has nearly outgrown. "Are you excited for school today?"

"What do you think?"

"You act just like your mother when she was your age. She didn't like it at all."

"Did you?"

"I loved it! Especially math," Bart answers excitedly.

"You're crazy, Papa. I guess that is why you're a good builder, though, isn't it?" she asks.

"Maybe so. Building anything does require math."

"I don't think I would like to be a builder."

"Why is that?"

"I don't like math."

"You like to paint."

"I love to draw *and* paint."

"Drawing and painting are a lot like building," Bart explains.

Cuori turns her head and looks up at her father's face. "But I don't use math to make art."

Bart chuckles at her seriousness and dislike of math. "No, not actively, but you are using it. Math is what we use to build images and identify structure within those images. You utilize math when creating or re-creating a scene from your mind." She feels the wonder and curiosity filling his tone as he speaks.

"So, I am a math genius?" she asks after thinking for a second.

"I think you are. You're so smart, you don't even realize you're using math."

Cuori giggles with her whole body. Then, she lies silently against him.

"I need to head to the shop, my darling. I will see you this evening."

"Okay. I love you," she says as they both stand from the chair.

Adele arrives from the bedroom in her nightgown, and Bart walks quickly toward her, hugging her tightly and whispering something inaudible in her ear before he kisses her goodbye for the day.

After Bart leaves, Adele and Cuori change their clothes, and Adele cooks eggs for breakfast. While the two eat, Adele says, "Can you walk to school with Luca today? Anna and Sheila are coming to help me in the garden this morning. We will walk back home with you from school, though, like usual."

"Okay," Cuori says, and her eyes light up with excitement. *Perfect!* she thinks.

"Well, *if* Anna and Luca show up. He might still be sick from whatever kept him from school yesterday," Adele adds. Almost as if on cue, there is a knock at the door.

"Come in!" Adele shouts from the kitchen.

Anna and Luca walk inside, both with their bright and sweet faces. Anna is always a big ball of optimism, which has worn off on her nine-year-old son.

"Hi, Aunt Anna!" Cuori greets.

"Hi, Cuori. Ooh, those eggs smell delicious."

"I made enough for you both," Adele says, covering her chewing mouth with her hand.

"Thank you." Anna serves herself and Luca the rest of the scrambled eggs and then joins Adele and Cuori at the table.

"Now, you have walked to school by yourselves before. I trust you can find your way again today. Adele and I don't want to have to go searching for you," Anna says with a laugh.

"Yes, Mama, we know how to get to school," Luca says, his big eyes beaming.

The dining room fills with chatter and laughs until everyone finishes their breakfast. Once finished, Adele and Anna kiss their kids goodbye, watching them from the front porch as they cross the street and begin their walk.

Cuori has known Luca her entire life and considers him to be like a little brother, even though he is actually a little older than her. They have few things in common, though. He has countless friends he plays with; none are like Cuori, so she immediately feels left out whenever it's more than just the two of them. She doesn't mind being left out. It gives her more time to watch people and daydream.

Walking to school with only Luca are her favorite days because she can slip away from him near the school entrance as he leaves her to join his friends. Today, she plans to be a few hours late for school. There is someone she wants to see.

When they arrive near the school entrance, Luca runs ahead into the building. A couple of teachers stand at the front doors talking amongst themselves, not seeing Cuori as she continues walking past them toward downtown Florence. Once she can no longer see the school, she retakes deeper breaths and steadies her pace. Other than the slight worry that Luca might have turned around and caught her walking away, delight fills her. He never looks back once he is with his friends though, she convinces herself. *Too easy.*

She dislikes keeping secrets from her parents, but if they were to discover that she sometimes skips school to visit her friend, Roald, she knows they would never let her see him again. She passes a couple of bars, empty in the morning but reeking of spilled alcohol from the night before. The neighborhood she must traverse to get to the city center is seemingly dirty and unsafe. Windows are broken in at least half the buildings; some doors hang on one hinge. She is on edge in these parts of the walk, scared of what she might see, but more afraid of how horrified her parents would be if they knew she was here alone. But seeing her friend is more than worth the risk. Besides, she has done this for a while now, and it seems danger is only awake at night; its aftermath is all that remains in the daytime.

After almost an hour of walking, she finally arrives at a busy city corner, a daily marketplace for various local and distant merchants. She quickly catches sight of a man sitting on the side of the street opposite her, holding a bucket. Happiness engulfs her. *Roald!*

She waits for a horse-drawn wagon to pass by and then darts across the brick street. She approaches Roald from behind. His face is downcast, so he doesn't notice her until she touches his hunched shoulder.

Barely fazed by her touch, he turns his head slowly. When his eyes land on Cuori, he straightens, and his face brightens with a rich smile. Roald is an old man with long gray hair and a messy, long beard. His clothes are filthy and patched, his face black with dirt, but Cuori only notices how it makes his smile all the more vibrant.

"Cuori, my friend!"

"Hi, Roald!" she says excitedly, then sits beside him on the edge of the street. "What are you doing today?"

"I'm just out here working again. I've got a couple of pieces of silver so far today."

"Good. Do you have enough to find a place to live and get a job yet?"

"Well, I almost did, but someone stole my bucket the other day, so now I have to start all over again."

"Oh no! Who stole it?" she asks, feeling angry at the thief.

"I think it was another homeless man down at the camp along the river like me. I'm not too worried about it, though. Whoever it was must have needed it more than me."

"Did you ask around? Maybe someone saw it be taken, and you could confront him," she suggests, sensing he hasn't even tried to find his money.

"Oh, sweet girl. That would be too convenient. Besides, sometimes in life, bad things happen, but you learn to keep going anyway, hoping that life will get better."

"You don't care about your money?"

"Sure, I do. But it's gone now..." Roald leans his head toward her as he lets his words hang in the air, then starts again. "There is no sense in getting upset about it. I will sit here as long as it takes to make it back."

"But you were so close," she says, confused.

"Young lady, one day you will understand that acceptance is a better way to live than denial. I don't want to spend my life fighting against circumstance but instead, accept life for what it is."

"Your life is awful," she says, immediately regretting it.

"Maybe if you compare it to someone else's, but this is all I've known for the majority of my life, so it's not too bad for me," Roald says with a lighthearted chuckle.

"I wish you could come live with us."

"I don't think your parents would like that, but I appreciate you thinking of me."

"When I have my own house one day, I will make a place just for you," she offers, feeling confident in her idea.

"That is the nicest offer anyone has given me. If I'm still alive when you have your own house, I'll finally have a home!" Roald's voice cracks.

"Yes! You'll still be alive. I need you to be," she says, scooting herself a few inches closer to him.

Roald puts his hand on her shoulder. "You don't need me. You are a special girl and will do well in life on your own."

"You are my only *real* friend," she admits.

"I doubt that. I'm sure all the kids at school love you. When you are there." Roald laughs.

"I think everyone likes me just fine, but nobody wants to be my friend."

"Why is that?"

"Because I am so different to other kids, I guess."

"I know what you mean. The more unique you are, the fewer people there are who understand you."

"Exactly, kids my age talk about bor—" She stops herself. "They don't talk about anything I'm interested in."

Roald smiles at her. "No, because you talk about big ideas. The things most people never make time to consider. A lot of kids aren't like you, but that is okay. You're different for a reason."

Cuori sits up. "Why do you think?"

"I can't tell you. You will have to figure it out for yourself," Roald says with his hoarse yet wise voice. "Perhaps you'll become the next great scientist or philosopher. Or both, like Galileo Galilei."

"That would be amazing!" she fantasizes. "But I'm not near as smart as he must have been."

He huffs at her. "Well, of course not yet. It might be impossible to see now, little one, but someday you will put to use all the unique pieces of yourself. Which could be the answer to some of the questions people have been asking for a millennium."

Cuori nods, but not because she has any true understanding, and changes the subject. "The painting I am working on for you is coming along well—I'll have it finished soon."

"I can't wait until it is done. It will be the best gift I have ever received!"

She smiles with contentment at her friend's compliment. The unlikely friends sit on the side of the busy city street and continue visiting like they usually do a few times a month. Roald is the only person besides her parents to whom she feels comfortable opening up, and the only other one who enjoys talking about philosophy. Her mother has no interest, and her father quickly relates any conversation back to music and math. His comfort topics.

She met him the first day she decided to skip school last year. A walk through downtown Florence to help the day pass by was rewarded with her first confrontation with a homeless person, who just happened to be one of the gentlest and most sincere people in all of Italy—at least in Cuori's opinion. Who knew an eight-year-old girl could form a bond with a seventy-year-old man based on spontaneous philosophical discussions?

"What are you going to do with the rest of your day?" she asks him.

"I'm going to sit here until I have—" Roald is cut off with surprise as someone drops three coins into his small bucket. "Well, Cuori, I'm going to buy us some candy. Let's go."

They stand from their seats on the dirty street and walk a short distance to a small shop selling a few hard candies and other common goods. Its colorfully decorated exterior creates an alluring environment for anyone with a sweet tooth.

On the weekend, these streets are lined with vendors selling fresh farm goods and endless bouquets of flowers. On Wednesdays, though, the streets and shops are less busy.

"We would like two of your biggest brown sugar cubes," Roald tells the woman behind the counter.

"That will be half a florin, Roald. Hi, Cuori!" she says, nodding to her.

"Hi, Miss Loui."

Roald pays for the candy, and they both stroll back outside. A rush of happiness fills her when the sugar kicks in after a couple of steps.

"It has been a treat seeing you today, Cuori, but I think it's time for you to head home. Don't you agree? The sun is at midday now."

"Okay. I wish I could see you every day," she complains.

"Yes, but then you might grow tired of me. This way, we always enjoy one another's company instead of taking it for granted," Roald says, patting her back. "Please be careful."

"I will. See you soon, Roald. I'll miss you." Her heart hurts when she has to leave him, but she is comforted, knowing she will return as soon as her and Luca have the opportunity to walk to school without their parents again. Which is happening more often as Adele becomes comfortable with it.

"Miss you too, bye for now," Roald says. She feels his eyes on her back until she is safely across the busy street. When she turns to wave goodbye again, his face has already disappeared. She sees only his long hair dancing in the breeze.

Her walk back to the school takes almost two times as long as it did this morning; at least, she feels like it does anyway. School is not her forte, but she manages to persevere through it somehow.

When she arrives at the school property, it is already the end of day recess, so she climbs over the short fence into the playground. The teachers never notice her sudden reappearance; they are always too busy chasing and disciplining the misbehaving kids. The students in her grade outnumber the understaffed teachers 20:1, meaning they hardly notice her absence, much less address it. Florence is growing and the church is trying to keep pace with its education services but is finding it difficult. There is one person she specifically tries to avoid, though. Luca. If he were to ever find out she was missing from school one day, he wouldn't hesitate to tell his mother.

After successfully being unnoticed, and waiting a few minutes at the picnic table, she sees her mother, Anna, and Sheila approaching the school. She finds Luca, and they meet their parents at the playground entrance, where Miss France lets them leave for the day.

Cuori and Luca lead the way home, and her mother and two friends follow behind. Guilt eats at her for not telling her mother that she skipped school again today, but then she remembers a part of a story she read some time ago. *Everyone has secrets.*

CHAPTER
Fifteen

Adele

*C*uori's golden pigtails fly in the afternoon breeze, capturing Adele's attention as they walk home from school. Her hair won't be so blond for much longer, she thinks. The auburn streaks are growing longer every day.

Cuori might be eight years old now, but she still sees her as the gift she was when she was born. Perhaps the miracle of her birth will always be what Adele sees first when she looks at her daughter. A miracle that must be protected at all costs—with love—she reminds herself. Careful to not smother her daughter. Although she worries Cuori feels stifled by her protective nature sometimes.

"So, the other day when Luca came home, I was in the middle of cooking and—"

"Dario brought you a big bouquet of roses!"

"Did I already tell this story?" Anna asks, surprised.

"Yes," Sheila says. "But it's okay. We know how special the moment was for you."

Adele smiles at her friends. Anna is a few years younger than her and is constantly filling in the silent spaces with anything she can think of. Sheila is much older than both of them and, in some ways, fills the role of an older sister. She has dry humor but does try to consider Adele and Anna's feelings.

"Oh, it was. It had been a long time since he showed me any attention. I think he might want to have another baby soon!"

Adele and Sheila squeal with excitement, causing Cuori and Luca to look back.

"You've been wanting this for so long!" Adele says.

"I know. I'm trying not to be too hopeful because nothing is actually confirmed, but I can hardly contain my joy!"

"Anna, you never contain your joy. Even if you only have a few drops, you share it with everyone!" Sheila says, and all three of them laugh.

When they arrive at Adele's home, Cuori and Luca head to her bedroom to play while the women gather around the kitchen bar for their afternoon snack and tea. Adele retrieves the glass jar sitting in the window, steeping tea by the warmth of the sun while Sheila and Anna slice and sprinkle tomatoes with basil and balsamic vinegar.

"The fruit of our labor," Anna toasts before taking a bite out of a tomato slice.

"Our reward for working in the garden all day," Sheila says.

"My reward is simply just working in the garden. I love it," Adele says.

"We know you're crazy, Adele, you don't have to tell us," Anna says, and she and Sheila giggle in agreement.

"I'm serious, though," she tries to explain. "Obviously, the fruit the garden produces is good, but I love the tending just as much as the harvest."

"And that is why Florence's largest and most beautiful garden is in *your* backyard," Sheila says.

"Exactly," she says.

"And that is also why it requires three women working almost every day to care for it," Anna adds.

"You love it, though, Anna," Adele teases.

"I love you two, and I'm really loving this tomato," Anna says, taking a bite. "But weeding... not so much."

Adele finishes her second slice and then meanders into the living room. "Gardening is like life, ladies. It's more about the journey than the outcome."

"Whatever you say, Adele," Sheila says, following behind her. Anna is the last to finish and make her way.

Over the last five years, Sheila, Anna, and Adele have spent most days with each other. For Anna and Adele, the friendship is easy to maintain, partly because they are both married, and their children are the same age. On the other hand, Sheila has no husband or children, yet she has become their best friend. Her candor and Anna's loquaciousness are delicately balanced by Adele's more modest nature.

Sheila's schedule is more challenging to maintain, though. She still works at the market on the weekend where she sells bread and some vegetables from Adele's garden. And she lives on the north end of Florence, a two-hour walk from the south-central section of the city where Adele and Anna live. Her home is in an old shack on a small plot of land she inherited from her father when she was young. A woman cannot legally own property in Italy, but because what she inherited is so tiny and the building worth so little, nobody—not even the government—cares to take it from her.

Adele knows that during the week, Sheila wakes up exceptionally early to walk the long distance to her house to help her and Anna in the garden each day. So she allows her to keep most of the profits earned from selling the produce from the garden.

"Have you read the paper recently?" Sheila asks.

"No. I try not to. Most of what is happening in Italy and other countries is depressing." Adele says.

"Well, I have kept up with it, and you're not wrong. Apparently, there is increasing political tension between a few city-states. Some journalists are predicting more war."

"I am so sick of war," Anna says. "Our parents and grandparents were in the midst of it and now here we are too. What is the purpose of it anyway?"

"Death," Adele answers.

"It's a way for those in power to try and keep or expand it. Killing innocent people in the process," Sheila says.

"Why can't men just be happy with what they have?" Anna asks.

"Anna, most men in this world are so foolish they would risk their lives and others' lives to satisfy their pride. And pride doesn't share; pride is never content; pride is an evil force which leads its host down increasingly dark paths," Sheila says, obviously familiar with the effects of pride on a person.

"Do you think women suffer from pride, too?" Adele asks Sheila.

"I don't know. A woman would have to have a seat of power first to test it. But I doubt we would suffer from it as badly as men, if at all."

Adele nods. Unsure she agrees, though.

"Why does anyone have to be in a seat of power?" The way Anna asks the question lets Adele know its level of meaning to her.

"You mean, why do we have leaders?" Adele asks, intrigued.

"Yeah. Why do we need certain figures to have power over us."

"Because if we didn't have leaders, society would be in chaos. Our cities would burn down," Sheila says, articulating a sort of chaos with her hands. "The ideal leader doesn't exercise power over his people but uses his power to protect us."

"I don't see why we need leaders. I mean, I know you two, myself included, wouldn't go into the city and start burning buildings because we don't have a leader. I think the majority of people are the same as us," Anna says.

"I was speaking figuratively about the city burning down," Sheila clarifies.

"Yes, so was I. I guess what I am asking is... would we still not be able to survive on our own and have respect for each human as we do now, or is that behavior dependent upon us being controlled by a person in power?"

"I see what you're asking now, and it's a good question." Adele takes a moment to consider before answering. "I think if everyone respected each other, we wouldn't need any form of government. But not everyone respects other people. And it only takes one to ruin it for everybody else," Adele says, remembering the man who attacked Sheila years ago.

"So, a good government should be established with only the purpose of protecting us from the people who don't want to live in harmony?" Anna asks.

"Yeah, in a perfect world," Sheila says.

"It seems as though the people who don't respect other people are the ones in seats of power." Adele voices her realization.

"I think women should start becoming leaders, and maybe all this war would finally stop," Anna says.

"Agreed," Sheila responds. "Sorry for bringing up so depressing a topic."

"No, it is good for us to be current on what is happening in our country. Another war would certainly affect our lives," Adele says.

"Absolutely," Anna says, her words lingering ever-so-slightly.

"What's wrong, Anna?" Sheila asks.

"I don't know for sure. Honestly, this world is a mess, and it scares me to bring another baby into it."

"Anna," Adele catches her glance, "bringing a new life into the world isn't something to be afraid of. It is the new life that can bring change to this war-filled time."

"But what if I can't protect my children against all the horrible things that could come?"

"You will protect your babies. Don't doubt yourself. Not even a hungry lion could get through you to them, much less another person." Adele laughs, and she's grateful when Anna and Sheila join her, loosening the tension in the air.

Sheila leans forward slightly to speak. "From what I can see, Anna, by *you* raising up a child, boy or girl, they will make the world a better place, not succumb to the evil already within it."

"Thank you both so much. Everything you said is so kind. I love you," Anna says with a wide smile.

"Love you too," Sheila and Adele chime in together as they wrap their arms around Anna for a moment.

"Anyone who inherits even a portion of your character, Anna, will be a blessing to everyone around them," Sheila adds.

The silence that fills the space around them invites Adele to share a secret, but then she quickly withholds it. *I'm not ready yet.*

It's Anna's talk of having another baby that jabs at Adele. She and Bart have tried to have another baby over the last five years, but she hasn't been pregnant once. But what if she confides in her friends? What if it would help her? She lifts her gaze. "I don't think I can have any more children," she says.

"Why do you say that?" Anna asks, her surprise and confusion showing in her expression.

"Because Bart and I have been trying for five years now."

Anna sighs with empathy.

"I'm so sorry." Sheila offers comfort. "I know how difficult it must be for you."

"I feel like a horrible person for being upset." Adele begins to cry. "Because we have Cuori, and she is perfect in every way, yet I'm acting like she isn't enough."

"You're not," Sheila says. "Wanting to have children is a natural desire that doesn't just leave a mother. And," she adds, "it in no way diminishes your love for the one you already have."

"It doesn't?" Adele asks.

"Not at all."

"Adele," Anna whispers. "The last *five* years? Why did you never tell us?"

Adele wipes away her lingering tears. "Because it is my own burden to bear with my husband. It isn't your problem to deal with."

"Are you crazy?" Anna raises her voice. "We are your friends. You are *my* friend, and I don't know what I would do without you. I tell you everything, and you help carry my struggles right along with me. I want to do the same for you."

"I understand why you held on to this yourself but promise me you will not carry this alone anymore. That is not a road you want to travel. Trust me. We are here, and we want to bear it with you," Sheila says softly but emphatically.

Adele feels a weight lifted from her heart and she loses more tears now, as do Sheila and Anna. "I'm sorry for not telling you until now, but I won't keep it to myself going forward."

"Good," Sheila says, hugging her.

"You are the strongest woman I know. You've been there for me in the midst of your own suffering. It's my turn to do the same for you," Anna says, holding her hand.

"Thank you. I needed this today, ladies," Adele says.

"Always," Sheila says. "How is Bart doing with all of this?"

"Fine, I think. We've both been disappointed, but honestly, it only increases our gratitude for the miracle we already have."

"Does he talk to anyone about it?" Sheila asks.

"Just me." *That I am aware of.*

"Does he talk about it much?"

"Not a lot, but enough, I'm sure. He has had a bad week at the shop, though."

"Why is that?" Anna asks.

"He has been working on this new instrument for nine years and has yet to make much progress. He was hoping this week was going to change that."

"It must be especially hard on him right now," Anna says.

"I think it has been. I've seen his excitement for work slowly fade away the last few years."

"That is how life works, though," Sheila says, leaning back in her chair, gaze loosening. "You find yourself excited about something and ready to go for it, but out of nowhere, something comes along and steals the excitement you once had and replaces it with despair."

"Nothing about being alive is fair. Most days are spent simply trying to survive," Adele says.

"The church taught me to pray to God when I was young. I used to believe that if I prayed hard enough for something, I would get what I wanted. I couldn't have been more of a fool. If God is real, He is a monster," Sheila says dryly.

"I prayed for Cuori," Adele says.

"I'm glad it worked out for you," Sheila says, not intending to be sarcastic but coming across as such.

She didn't mean it like that, Adele tells herself.

"I prayed for friends many years ago," Anna says, widening her arms to encompass Adele and Sheila. "I couldn't have found better ones."

Sheila wears a defeated expression. "Maybe God just hates me then."

"God doesn't hate you or anyone else. We are His children, living in a broken world. One where we don't always get what we want or ask for. You might not have received what you asked God for, but you were His answer to what someone else asked for," Anna says, smiling brightly.

Sheila can't help but smile now, too. "You two are the best."

Adele smiles and laughs with them, always filled with gratitude for the friends she has found, who have made Florence finally feel like home.

CHAPTER
Sixteen

Bart

*M*ost days in his shop, Bart is productive. Either meticulously working on the pianoforte frame, which will house the strings and hammer action system, or developing the action itself. Today, though, he is contemplating where he is going wrong in attaching the hammers to the keys.

In order for the hammer to strike the string, the key itself must be pressure sensitive, which required a complex set of balancing weights to be attached to the hammer, but yesterday, when he tested his latest adjustment, the key became stuck in a pressed position when playing mezzo-forte or greater. Running his eyes over the complex arrangement of what will be the instrument's inner workings, he can't conceive of a single other solution. He's tried everything, which has led to losing confidence that he will ever figure it out. It is only by remembering what Adele told him last night—that it wasn't about the instrument itself but the impact it would make on the people who would hear the melodies created by it—that he is able to continue believing in his ability to find the answer.

By late afternoon, though, all he has managed to do is to think endlessly, other than his pacing, of course, which helps him process the multitude of emotions coursing in his brain. *What else can I try?* he keeps asking himself but to no avail.

"How is the greatest inventor of the seventeenth century doing today?" Andy speaks as he walks into the room.

Andy is always in a positive mood, and thankfully so. Otherwise, Bart would seriously doubt his job security.

"I don't know who that guy is, but I'm doing alright."

Andy approaches Bart and places a hand on his shoulder, his white wig worn as awkwardly yet prestigiously as ever. He only wears it on days he is meeting someone important or is traveling. It highlights his prominent nose. Andy looks at the action system Bart has built. "Tested it anymore today?"

"I haven't. I've thought of a million different solutions, though."

Andy steps back, leaning on an opposing table. "You're not being hard on yourself, right?"

"No. Well, no more than I deserve," he clarifies.

"There is no reason whatsoever to take this hammer action's failure to work and use it to beat yourself up. This is a part of creating something new. It requires testing over and over again, and most tests will be failures," Andy says. "But you already know all this."

"So far, everything I have tried with this instrument has been a failure. I don't know..." Bart trails off, looking at the floor.

"You don't know what?"

Bart scratches his short, scruffy beard and after a considering moment, he says what's in his mind. "I don't know if I'll ever be able to do this."

Andy stops leaning against the table and stands upright. "Why do you say that?" he asks coolly.

Bart holds Andy's gaze. "I have been here the majority of a decade. It will be nine years in a few months. Look around at what I have accomplished. Nothing. Obviously, you picked the wrong person." It hurts his heart to admit it, but it is what he has been thinking for a while now.

"You are the one who built the two-keyboard harpsichord, right?" Andy asks.

"Yes," he answers, unsure why Andy changed the subject.

"You advanced the capabilities of the harpsichord entirely on your own, by your own vision, right?"

"Yes."

"How long did it take you?"

"About seven years. But I was also building and selling harpsichords at the time while working on the more advanced one. It was mostly a fun project. My income didn't depend on it," Bart says, admitting another rising fear.

"It doesn't matter. It took you seven years to build a new type of harpsichord, an instrument *already* invented. The foundation for your work was already completed. But you complain about the pianoforte taking a long time to build when it is an entirely new instrument, an entirely new concept. You have started from scratch, so commonsense says it can reasonably take seven years, even fourteen years, perhaps more," Andy says with conviction.

"Isn't that too long?" Bart asks.

"Have I ever put a time constraint or expectation on you?"

"No."

"That is because this is your job until you are *finished*. I do not care how long it takes."

Andy's confirmation of job security and his understanding of
the time required to create an entirely new instrument puts Bart's
mind at ease, and he's gratified, too, that Andy isn't disappointed.
"Okay," he says.

"It's alright to be frustrated with yourself sometimes, but don't
stay there, Bart. You are brilliant, and you will finish the pianoforte.
It will be your mark on the world," Andy says.

There it is again—my impact on the world.

"Thank you. If I can finish this—"

"When," Andy cuts in.

Bart smiles. "*When* I finish this, I believe your idea for an instrument might change music forever."

"You have no idea. My dreams have only grown since we began
this project. The pianoforte will change *everything.*"

A minuscule spark of inspiration flashes up Bart's spine. To
think of it in those terms, that he is sharing in an endeavor that
will change the world gives him hope. He knows now that he isn't
wasting his time. "I'm just glad I get to be a part of it," he says.

"Part of it?" Andy sounds incredulous. "You are the creator of
it," he says emphatically, and heading out of the shop, he shouts,
"See you tomorrow."

Moments later, once Bart collects his thoughts and the remainder of his bread loaf from lunch, he leaves the shop, too. On his
way out of the music hall, the sound of the violin catches his ear.
Following the melody toward the entrance of the main building
that houses the auditorium, he peeks around the doorway and
recognizes Frank. The violinist, who is usually gone by this time,
has his back to Bart. The way he moves his body in sync with his
arm makes the instrument sing. Bart is captivated. Frank is so dramatic when he plays.

The tune is in a minor key now, projecting vibrations into the air so rich in emotion and character that Bart could melt into tears. "That was beautiful, Frank," Bart says when Frank finishes, and he's dismayed when the man jerks around, flinging his arms and gasping. Frank manages to hold his violin secure, but his bow isn't so lucky and gets flung nearly ten feet away, landing near Bart.

"Shit," Frank cries out. "You scared me."

"Sorry." Bart laughs. "What is the name of the tune you were playing?"

Frank recomposes himself. "It doesn't have a name yet."

"Did you write it?"

"Well, in my mind. Do you think it's good enough to write down?"

"More than good enough. I was on the verge of crying just standing here," Bart compliments.

"Really?" Frank asks, surprised. "I have only ever played written music so far into my career. Never wrote it."

"Why not?"

"I have never viewed myself as a composer, I guess," Frank admits.

"What I heard just now is comparable to what I've heard Andy and Antonio play."

Franks's eyes beam, and his wide mouth turns into a huge smile. "Thank you, Bart. That means so much, especially coming from you. You know music better than anyone."

Bart frowns. "Me? I can only play the harpsichord and guitar enough to know whether their sound is good. You all can play *any* instrument remarkably well."

"Yeah, but you *build* instruments. You know how to make them produce the most perfect sounds. None of us can do what you do," Franks says as he finds a stool and sits.

"It takes a variety of talents to make music possible, it seems," Bart says.

"Very true, and this place is full of talent. Sometimes I feel like an imposter."

"Yeah, right. If you're an imposter, then everyone here is too," Bart says, and they both laugh. "Especially me."

"This place is almost like a dream. I constantly doubt myself. I'm worried I'll wake up one day and find out none of it is real."

"Trust me. I know what it is to doubt oneself. I have learned that in great measure over the last few years."

"I'm glad I'm not alone," Frank says.

"So, you were just making up that tune as you went along?" he asks, returning to the subject of Frank's impressive composition.

"Yes. I started in G major, then shifted to E minor, which added a lot of emotion. I'm a sucker for emotionally heavy melodies. Or emotionally rich, depending on who you ask."

An image of Adele suddenly forms in Bart's mind, and he is seized with an idea. "Frank, I have a request for you. If you're okay with it."

"What is it?"

"Adele's birthday is coming up in a couple of weeks. Could you write a tune? Then I bring her here and you play it for her?"

It is a moment before Frank responds, and when he does, he says, "No."

"No problem, sorry." Bart feels the heat of embarrassment crawl over his face and ducks his chin, hoping Frank won't see his discomfort. The silence becomes awkward.

Frank breaks it. "I will not write a tune, but I will *help* you write one and play it *with* you for her."

Bart looks up at Frank.

He smiles again. "It'd be weird for just me to play a tune for your wife," he says and picking up a guitar, he walks over to Bart and hands it to him. He bends down to retrieve the violin bow he threw earlier on his way back to the music stand.

"Okay," Bart says, and carrying the guitar to the center of the room, he sits on a stool facing Frank. "Just so you know, Frank, I have no idea how to write a tune," he laughs.

"It's much simpler than you think," Frank says, taking up his violin again. "I want you to pick any chord progression and repeat it over and over. Then I'll come in, letting the violin be the voice."

"Right now?"

"Yeah, start when you're ready!"

Bart ponders, wondering how to begin, in what key? What sort of chord progression?

"Just start with C," Frank says as if he has read the panic running through Bart's mind.

"Okay," he says. "I can do that." Bart strums the guitar, and the familiar and comforting tone of C speaks vibrantly throughout the room.

After a bit, Frank says, "Try A minor now."

Bart reforms his left-hand grip on the guitar, and the sound vibrating across the room changes to A minor's tense yet beautiful tone.

"Now F."

He does as Frank instructs, shifting the ambiance of the room once more.

"G."

The last chord change to G puts the icing on the cake for Bart and he grins broadly.

"I told you it was simple. Now, keep playing that same progression at 4/4 time, and I will try to form a melody."

"Got it." Bart continues playing the easy chord progression, tapping his foot to keep time, and when Frank slowly begins forming long, elegant notes out of his rhythm and chord changes, his heart lifts. The two instruments mesh together brilliantly, creating harmony and a melody so smooth and opulent that he closes his eyes, losing himself in it. He is aware enough to keep strumming the chords even as he experiences the tune as if he were only a listener, one who is completely captivated.

It is Frank's style of play, Bart thinks in some portion of his brain. It is both worshipful and romantic, and in its creation, he knows it is a perfect tribute to his beautiful and lovely Adele. As the melody becomes more fully developed, the sound from both instruments swells to its loudest capacity, filling the room. It is invisible, but behind his closed eyes, Bart sees it in bold and palpable color.

Now as Frank's playing slows and softens, Bart follows his lead, doing the same, and together they gently bring the tune to an end. A pleasing harmony of final notes lingers, an echo that drifts through the room and then a hush that to Bart feels almost reverent.

He is slow to waken from what feels like a magical spell, and when at last he takes his hand from the guitar it is to wipe away a small water of tears on his cheek.

"What did you think?" Frank asks, setting down his violin. He settles on the stool facing Bart.

"I have no words. It is far more than I was imagining."

"I'm glad you like it. We played it through enough times. I should easily remember the melody, but I'll write it down before I go home."

Bart rises from his perch, still experiencing ethereal feelings as he returns the guitar to the place where he'd watched Frank pick it up. "Thank you, Frank," he says, turning to the violinist. "I have never played a tune like that before, much less participated in *writing* one."

"Brilliant, isn't it?"

"I'm so excited. I feel like a child opening a gift." He swallows and takes a deep breath, looking around the room in amazement. When he returns his attention to Frank, he says, "I needed this tonight,"

"I'm glad I could help, but it was *your* idea," Frank says with a lighthearted laugh.

"I cannot wait to play it for Adele!" Bart sits back down on the stool.

"You think she will like it?" Frank says as he leans over and stretches his arm out to place the violin in its stand.

"No," he says, and when Frank looks back at him with some mix of shock and disappointment, Bart smiles. "She will *love* it."

[Listen to 'Adele's Gift']

CHAPTER
Seventeen

1695 – Cuori
Five Years Later

*T*he sunlight glistens in her eyes, reflecting as it peeks through her bedroom curtains. Her gaze is fixed upon a canvas, where paintbrush strokes come together, forming a detailed image of a woman's face. Cocking her head to one side, Cuori concentrates on the path of the paintbrush, and speaking to her subject, she says in a low voice, "You are a woman in a painting, not a real person." But somehow, in her heart, Cuori feels differently. Considering the placement of freckles and skin tags on the woman's face, one could assume the picture is more real than even Cuori can convince herself otherwise.

After she adds the final line of the forehead, her mother knocks on her door. "Luca is here. Time to go."

Satisfied, Cuori drops her brush into a jar of water, and leaving her room, she and Luca say goodbye to their mothers. Now that both are of some age, they talk a bit more on their daily walk to school, although Cuori feels she is the more mature and sophisticated of the two. Luca behaves like the average thirteen-year-old boy. He's childish in ways Cuori is not. She often thinks she is like an older sister to him.

"Did you see the fight yesterday in the kitchen?" Luca asks with bubbling excitement.

"No."

"How could you have missed it? It was so fun. Some kids started throwing food, but Miss France stopped them before it got too messy."

Cuori looks sidelong at Luca. "Really? Some kids, huh?"

Luca's smile is chagrined. "Fine. I was the one who started throwing food, but the rest of my table started as soon as I did."

She laughs at him, and he does, too. "You call that fun?" Cuori asks sarcastically. "Did anyone get hurt before it was stopped?"

"Romeo got a bloody nose. That is all I could see anyway."

"How? You said it was food being thrown."

"I'm not sure how, but Romeo is a bully. My friends speculated someone punched him when he was distracted as payback."

"He's that one big kid, right?" Cuori asks.

"Yeah, he's huge."

"I didn't know he was a bully."

"He is. He is nice to girls, though," Luca says.

"He is older than us. How do you know that about him?" Cuori eyes Luca curiously.

"Because he is mean to me," Luca finally says, flat-voiced.

"I'm sorry, Luca. I never knew. Does he hurt you?"

"He doesn't touch me, but he says mean things."

Cuori's heart breaks for Luca. She's always felt protective of him. "What does he say?"

Luca watches his feet. "He tells other kids I like boys instead of girls and tells me that is why I have no friends. But I do like girls, and I have a lot of friends!"

"He is obviously jealous." And he's going to regret picking on Luca, Cuori adds in her mind even as a small fire ignites in her chest.

"Jealous?"

"Yeah. He's envious of how many friends you have so he says mean things to you to make himself feel better. And," Cuori adds, "I bet *he* is the one who likes boys instead of girls."

"Seriously?" Looking at Cuori, Luca grins. "How do you know?"

"I read books and stories."

"I don't like to read," Luca admits.

"Yeah, I know. I don't understand how," Cuori says.

"It is so boring."

"You're just crazy." Skipping ahead a few steps, she says, "Want to race to school?" She takes off, not waiting for his answer.

Luca quickly follows suit, yelling, "You started before me, cheater." He is a small-framed boy, having not yet hit a growth spurt, and his knapsack—half his size—flails around him as he runs.

Cuori beats him to the school entrance. "You're slow."

"You cheated," he repeats breathlessly, then, as usual, he walks past her as if she were invisible to join his friends.

Sisters are embarrassing to young boys, she thinks as she watches him for a moment. Luckily, he never even looks back before entering the school. Slipping behind the building, she follows what is now a familiar route to downtown Florence, one that she knows like the back of her hand. She receives a warm and non-invasive smile from almost everyone she encounters as she walks. Nothing has changed about the seedy buildings she passes by, though, except the newly replaced windows of some of the taverns. The church and city have started enforcing more property maintenance laws in an attempt to keep Florence up to its high standards of beauty as people expect one of the largest and most successful cities in all of Europe to be.

The click of horse hooves mingles with the clatter of wagon wheels rolling on the brick roads and bounces off the buildings as Cuori draws closer to the square. Just before arriving at the busy intersection, where she usually finds Roald, she stops to lean over the edge of the street overlooking the river that connects Florence to the rest of Italy and splits the city into two parts. The Arno River is always full of canoes carrying goods from one city to another. She enjoys watching them and waving at the occupants as they pass by. A few even wave back.

Leaving the bridge, she looks around for Roald. He is never in the exact same spot but is usually in this area. Darting across the street, she continues looking until her glance lands on a man wearing dark clothes, sitting on the sidewalk and leaning against a building. Although he has a hood over his head, she knows it's Roald.

Approaching Roald, she finds him asleep. Rather than nudging him awake, she settles down beside him, taking visual inventory of his belongings. She recognizes most of them, the worn-out leather bag made for a saddle and the canvas with a field of wildflowers painted on it—the one she gave him five years ago. It has only a few black streaks despite spending its life on the streets of Florence like Roald.

Now, as Cuori nudges him with her elbow, his light snoring stops abruptly. At first, he gazes curiously at the surrounding world before turning to look at Cuori. "Oh," he huffs. "Sorry. I didn't see you, Cuori."

"It's okay. Sorry to interrupt your nap."

"You didn't interrupt me. I take naps all day." He chuckles, the wrinkles on his face revealing his seventy-five years of age and the unkindness of life.

"Hungry?" she asks.

"Always."

Cuori opens her small school bag and pulls out the lunch her mother made for her. "Here you go."

"Thank you. You know you don't have to take care of me," he says with a grateful smile and soft eyes.

"Yes, I do. You're my friend. Who else would anyway?"

Through a mouthful of bread, Roald says, "You're the only one."

Cuori's heart fills up with joy at Roald's dependency on her. She feels responsible for him and is glad to fill the void he has in his life. "I'm happy to be the one who takes care of you. It makes me feel special."

"You are special without the part of taking care of me. And I am the one who feels special. Blessed, actually."

"Blessed?"

"Yeah," Roald says, licking his fingers free of food remnants.

"Doesn't blessed mean getting stuff from God?" She sits both shoulders against the wall of the building, but keeps her head turned toward him.

"Not at all."

"Well, that is what the priest at church says it is," Cuori says confidently, doubting Roald's reasoning. Her family's faithfulness to the church reveals itself in her.

"Being blessed is a state of mind. An ability to be grateful for what you have."

"But you have nothing," Cuori quickly reminds him.

Roald locks her gaze. "Cuori, I have everything. I have life."

She gazes back at him, intrigued by the lines of his face. "But you don't have a home or family, and you are always hungry. I would be mad at God if I were you."

"I don't conform well to social classes or expectations, and because of this, I am without dependable food and shelter, and my family has either passed away or disowned me. But I am still *alive*. I still see the sunrise and sunset, which is reason enough for me to wake up each day. And I have you as a friend who makes some days *extra* special," Roald says, bumping his shoulder against hers.

"You're unbelievable," Cuori says, shaking her head.

"Probably. But crazy people make life interesting. If everyone were the same, we would all be bored out of our minds," Roald says, causing both of them to chuckle. "One of these days, Cuori, I will tell you about my family and how I ended up where I am."

She leans forward from the side of the building and her face sparks with curiosity. "Why can't you tell me now?"

"Because you will understand it better when you are a little older."

"Fine," she says, disappointed, but only momentarily. "I want to be like you when I grow up."

"Homeless, no family, and always hungry?" Roald asks with a smirk.

Cuori's face turns red with embarrassment. "I'm sorry for saying that."

"Why? It's true." Roald laughs.

"I want to be happy, even if I have nothing," she says seriously.

"Ahh. You want to know the secret?"

"What is it?"

"Smile all the time, nap when you get tired, and watch people."

"Seriously?" Cuori asks with a doubtful tone.

"Absolutely. Smiling boosts your mood, sleeping keeps you healthy, and people are entertaining."

She nods, thinking she agrees with the last one.

Roald continues, "Watching people will also reveal that having many belongings doesn't always make you happy."

"Huh. Sounds easy," she says, pulling away strands of her wavy auburn hair that a sudden breeze has blown across her face.

"It is easy. Life shouldn't be so hard," Roald says, stretching his arms into the air and shifting himself to a more comfortable position on the hard-brick ground.

A brief silence fills the space between them. Cuori breaks it. "Roald?"

No response.

She leans forward and, looking into his face, she finds he has fallen asleep. Well, she thinks, he is old and needs his rest. She jumps up from the ground, tucks his belongings in close to him, and leaves him alone to sleep.

♩♪🎹♪♫

The sun isn't even halfway across the sky before Cuori heads back toward the school. Time spent with Roald is increasingly shorter than usual. She has found him asleep more often than not when she has come to visit in the last year. His body is beginning to show much more age.

Since she was left with more time remaining than usual before she needed to return to school, she decided to take a long way back, exploring more of the city and learning the location of interesting businesses and city offices. One of the buildings she walks by is the Florentine Court—the music hall—where her father works. She passes by it quickly. To be recognized by anyone would undoubtedly lead to her father finding out. *I have kept skipping school a secret for this long, and I don't want to risk losing it now.*

She strolls past horse barns, wood and metalworking shops, brickmakers, and a glassblowing factory. Florence is certainly not short on its manufacturing capacity. She continues to another block. This one has flower shops, leather stores, and busy cafés. The smell of steeping tea, freshly crushed coffee beans, and blooming flowers overtakes her nostrils, blocking the usual smell of horse manure.

She sits at an empty table in front of one of the cafés, admiring the shoppers and store owners sweeping and tending to their buildings' entrances. A basket of petunias larger than her whole body also absorbs much of her attention. *Mama would love these!*

As she is swept up in her discovery of Third Street, two men walking along the opposing sidewalk stop and stare at her. She doesn't notice them until they are halfway across the street with four eyes locked on her. Of all the years she has spent walking to downtown Florence, she has never encountered anyone with bad intentions, so she gives them the benefit of the doubt. When she realizes they are headed toward her and still staring, she looks away, hoping they will pass her by. Their shadows grow closer, and she feels her pulse kicking up a notch.

When they approach her, the shorter man with a full beard says, "Hi, little lady. Are you alone?" His lack of wrinkles on his face tells her he is quite young despite his beard and voice making him seem older.

"Yes," she says with quick eye contact. Something about the way his posture adjusts tells her she has made a mistake by admitting she was alone.

Now, the taller man with squinted eyes says, "Why don't you come with us then? You shouldn't be alone."

"No, I'll stay here for now. Thank you, though." This is not good, she thinks, feeling heat overtake her whole body.

"Aw, you are a sweet thing, but I wasn't asking," the tall one says.

"Please leave me alone," she says shakily.

The short one steps closer. "Don't make a big scene, darling. We only want you to walk with us. We will keep you safe."

When he moves closer it unlocks her defenses and her voice gains strength. "You think I am an idiot? You are creeps. Leave me alone," she says with a demanding tone.

"I like feisty girls, but you're starting to test our patience," the tall man says, also stepping closer. Their shadows hang over her like fear.

"If you don't leave now, I'm going to scream. And I can scream *really* loud," she says, hoping to deter them. Feeling foolish for thinking so.

"You wouldn't do that," the short one says, almost drooling as his gaze continues to be fixed on her.

She fills her lungs with air and prepares to scream at the top of her lungs, but before she can, she hears a man from behind the two standing over her say, "What is going on here?"

She can't see his face, but his voice is somehow familiar.

The short man answers with a stutter, "Uh, this girl is all alone, so we are trying to help her." They step aside a few inches, opening up a space for Cuori to have a partial view of the other man. She can tell he is wearing a white wig, but cannot see his face.

Cuori's frightened eyes and adrenaline-filled veins must reveal the two men's true intent because the other man says, "No, you need to leave now."

The two would-be kidnappers and assaulters quickly step back and walk away. When they no longer block her view, Cuori sees the face of a man she knows well, and her heart drops. *Andy.*

CHAPTER
Eighteen

Cuori

*S*he has never felt so conflicted when trying to choose joy or fear as she looks into Andy's eyes. Her heart still pounds even though the two men, who were standing over her, are long gone. Andy keeps his distance a few feet away, looking at her with his quiet composure. Probably trying to recognize her accurately. "Cuori?"

"Yes," she says.

"I thought it was you." He takes a seat across from her. "Have you eaten lunch?"

Andy is a kind and gentle man, but looking at him in this setting requires all her strength. *I am going to be in so much trouble.* "No," she answers him.

He waves a waitress over to their table and orders a small sandwich for each of them. Andy doesn't open a dialogue once the waitress is gone, and Cuori appreciates the silence. It allows her time to reflect on the potential reactions her parents might have on learning of her skipping school.

"Are you going to tell me what you're doing here this time of day?" Andy finally says.

"I was walking to school," she answers honestly.

"School will be finished soon." Andy cocks an eyebrow.

"Back to school," she clarifies.

"The school is on the opposite side of the city. A long walk, likely an hour for you," he says.

"I was exploring the city because school is boring to me. I planned to be back there before it was over for the day like I usually do."

"You usually do?"

"Most days. The ones my mama allows me and Luca to walk ourselves," she admits. The urge to lie is strong, but she knows it would be useless.

Andy sits back in his chair, crossing his arms. "I see. When did this start?"

"Are you going to tell my papa?" She blurts the question, leaning forward, her whole body shaking.

"I asked you a question first. We will get to yours later," he responds calmly.

"When I was seven," Cuori says defeatedly, and she expects Andy to be surprised, but if he is, he hides it well.

Andy lets only a bit of surprise scurry across his face. "You've been bored of school since you were seven?"

"Yes."

"Do you pass your tests? I assume you attend enough to take them." He smirks.

"Yes. They are easy." She sits back now. Andy's seeming lack of judgment or disapproval allows her to relax a little.

"Now, if you aren't at school often, how do you know the answers to the questions on the tests?"

"I read."

"Oh yes. I know that." Andy nods. "I've sent most of the books I own home with your father, and when he brings them back, he always tells me you want more. You love to paint too, right?" he asks.

"Reading, drawing, *and* painting."

"He showed me a painting you created of a scene where people were standing in line at the market. It was stunning. I could almost recognize some of the faces within it. You are a talented artist, Cuori." He falls silent as the waitress approaches and serves their hot sandwiches. When they have finished their lunch, and Andy has paid for it, he turns to Cuori. "Care if I walk you to school?"

She shakes her head, thinking she will enjoy his company. Or, thinking he's only doing it because he doesn't trust her.

"So, are you going to tell my papa?" she asks, looking up at Andy.

He keeps his gaze forward. "You are a bright young girl. What do you think I should do? As a friend of your father."

Cuori drops her glance. "You should tell him."

"I disagree." A beat. "*You* should tell him and your mother."

The spark of hope that ignited in her mind falls into a bucket of cold water. "You think *I* should tell them?" she asks in disbelief.

"Yes."

"Why?"

"Cuori, you told me you skip school regularly. It doesn't seem to impair your education, but as you learned today, it does put you in the way of danger."

"This was the first time anyone ever acted like they wanted to hurt me. I promise," she says, trying to be convincing.

"They weren't acting, Cuori. Those were dangerous men."

"But it has never happened before," she explains.

"It only takes one time. If I had not been there, they could have taken you away and hurt you in unimaginable ways before anyone else would even notice and come to help you. Do you realize the danger you put yourself in by being alone?"

She lowers her head, embarrassed. "Yes, sir."

"Then I will let you be the one to explain to your parents what has been going on."

They continue their walk without saying anything more, but Cuori can't help but think about Roald and how she might not see him again, at least not for a while. Her throat thickens with tears at the thought of losing her friend and, soon, she can't keep them inside. The sobs break from her chest.

Andy stops, and bringing his gaze level with hers, he says, "You are a smart and brave girl. You know your parents will not punish you harshly. They love you so much."

She just nods. To tell him about Roald would be too difficult to explain.

They finally arrive at the school entrance. Cuori's tears have dried on the outside, but her sorrow is a weight inside her. "You can leave me here. I know how to get in, so they won't know I've been gone."

He nods. "Be careful."

"I will," she says. "Thank you."

"You're welcome. I'm glad our paths crossed today."

She forces a smile.

"And Cuori," he says.

She turns, looking back at him.

"I'll know if you tell them or not."

She nods and enters the school unnoticed, only moments before they are released for the day.

Luca talks for the entirety of their walk home. Tuning him out, she replays the events of her day, thoughts running a fruitless circle in her mind. If only she hadn't gone exploring after leaving Roald. If only she'd returned to school immediately. She knows Andy's right, that her parents won't punish her harshly. What she is afraid of, though, is their disappointment. She could count on one hand the number of times her father has spanked her or when her mother grabbed her ear. They wouldn't be mad, just sad, which always makes Cuori feel much worse.

Beside her, Luca stops abruptly, breaking Cuori's thought.

"Why is he here now?" Luca says.

Cuori stares ahead in the direction Luca is looking and she sees the paper man heading their way, tossing a rolled newspaper onto the walkway of each house he passes.

"The news is never delivered this late in the day," Luca says.

"You're right," Cuori says.

They step off the path as the man approaches, and he hustles by them without a word. When he is out of sight, Cuori picks up one of the newspapers.

"That is someone else's paper, Cuori," Luca says nervously.

"I'm only looking really quick," she says. At first, the bold heading that catches her attention shocks her, but within moments it sends an angry fire through her veins.

No. 182587

Florence Daily News

SATURDAY 23, JUNE, 1695

CRISTOFORI EXPOSED AS A FRAUD:
AN INCAPABLE INVENTOR
See Pg 2

CHAPTER
Nineteen

Adele

*A*t Adele's home, tension consumes the air where she and Anna sit on the front porch, waiting for Cuori and Luca to make it back from school. Impatience and anger flood through her, desperately wanting to be released. Sheila has already left for the day, and Anna will leave with Luca as soon as they arrive.

"I just cannot believe this." Adele sighs. "Journalists are nothing but piles of shit!"

"It was the newspaper who published it," Anna says.

"Newspapers are piles of shit!" Adele says, looking at Anna to see if she is more satisfied with her phrasing.

"I'm sorry, Adele. I hope all of this is straightened out quickly."

"Oh, it will be. I'll drag whoever wrote this garbage out of their house and onto the street," she says threateningly, waving today's paper in the air. Her kind and modest nature are nowhere to be found.

Anna cocks her head to the side, and in what Adele guesses is an attempt to lighten the mood, says, "You don't mean that."

Adele glares at her.

"Okay. Maybe you do."

The women stand up when they catch sight of Luca and Cuori and bid each other a hasty goodbye.

Cuori joins Adele and, watching Anna and Luca walk away, she says, "What is going on? Why aren't they staying?"

Adele cuts her off. "Put your bag away. We have to go see your father."

"Is this because of the newspaper?" Cuori asks.

"Yes. Hurry." Adele opens the door and Cuori scoots past her, rejoining her on the front porch only seconds later.

"Why did they say papa is a fraud?" Cuori asks as they set out toward the music hall.

"I don't know. But it makes me mad."

"Me, too."

Adele looks at her daughter, who is nearly at eye level with her now. "I'm sorry. It's not good to be mad. I'm annoyed."

"Mama. It's okay to be angry sometimes."

"Okay. This time is fine. This time, we can punch someone!" Adele shouts.

"Really?"

"No. I didn't mean that." *I'm going crazy.* "We are going to see your father because he will need our support." Her anger paces her mind like a ferocious lion wanting to leap from its cage, but for the sake of her daughter, she fights it back. Memories of Cuori's past anxieties remind her not to overwhelm her daughter. To protect her from uncontrollable emotions like when she was a child. *Don't dump your stress on her,* she tells herself.

"Do you think people will be mean to him if they believe the newspaper?" Cuori asks.

"They could. That is why he shouldn't have to face them alone. We live in a world where the opportunity to hurt someone and slander their name is a form of entertainment for a lot of people."

"Why would anyone find that entertaining?" Cuori asks.

"Drama and gossip are the common and preferred ways to pass the time. You'll see when you grow older, you'll even be tempted to participate."

"I will never."

"Good. You are strong-willed." She manages an authentic and proud smile. Their pace slows slightly, as the tension releases with conversation.

"Have you ever gossiped?" Cuori asks her.

Adele sighs and looks into the distance, then glancing at her daughter, she says, "Yes. Quite a few times. This is why I know how people act. I am one of them."

"Oh."

"I do not gossip anymore, though, and am always careful not to fall back into it. I know how words can hurt people, and I do not want to hurt people." She thinks of when she first met Sheila.

She notices Cuori's lack of response and finds it unsettling. When Cuori doesn't respond, Adele looks at her, thinking how unlike her it is to be so quiet. "Is everything okay?"

Cuori doesn't meet Adele's gaze, but stares at the ground in front of her. "Mama?"

"Yes."

"I have to tell you something."

Adele takes Cuori's arm, and stopping her, tips her chin to look into her eyes. "What is wrong, Cuori?"

Cuori's face floods with tears, which hinder her ability to speak. Adele pulls her in close, pressing her daughter's head against her chest as though she were still only three. "Talk to me."

"You're going to be mad." Cuori barely gets the words out.

"I could never be mad at you, my love."

"I haven't been going to school."

Adele's heart pauses. "What? What do you mean?"

"I have been skipping school to walk around the city during the day."

Adele continues to rub Cuori's back and hold her close. Staring into the middle distance, she tries to make sense of her daughter's confession. It can't be true, can it? She would have known, wouldn't she?

"Please don't hate me, Mama."

"My love, I do not hate you." She peels Cuori from her chest and cupping her face, she tips her forehead to Cuori's. "I could never hate you. I am confused. Very confused. But we can talk about this with your father, later."

"Are you disappointed in me?"

"No. Why would you think that?"

"Because I lied to you and Papa."

"Like I said, I am confused, but neither I nor your father could ever be disappointed in you. You are my daughter, and I will always only love you." She pulls her back into a hug. "Thank you for telling me," Adele says even as she thinks the timing couldn't be worse. "Come," she says. "We must see to your father."

They set out again, walking at a faster pace now to make up for the lost time. Adele is attempting to be both brave and gentle at the same time. A supporter and defender of her husband but a loving and kind mother. She feels qualified for neither at the moment as she tries to figure out how her daughter has managed to skip school without her finding out about it.

They round one last corner before arriving at the entrance of the music hall, the largest building in view. Always spectacular. They must wait a few moments before crossing the busy, wagon-filled street. Finally, a clearing opens and they run across.

Bart's shop is through the music hall, all the way to the back of the building. Adele hears no music being played as they enter, but a few musicians are clustered at the front of the stage. Intent on getting to her husband, Adele does not stop to visit.

"Adele!" a man calls.

Turning, she finds herself looking into Andy's kind and sparsely wrinkled face. "Andy," she replies and hugs him.

He divides his glance between Adele and Cuori. "My favorite two ladies. What brings you here?"

"Nothing good, sadly." She holds up the newspaper and watches as Andy reads the bold headline and takes in its meaning.

His mouth flattens in disgust. "This is not right." He takes a few deep breaths, then more calmly, he says, "Please know this is false. I am going to talk to Scipione now."

Adele detects a hint of nervousness in his tone. Ignoring it, she says, "Bart will be devastated. What should we do?"

"I need to leave now to catch Scipione before his office closes. I'll talk to Bart tomorrow. But you can be sure, and you can assure Bart, that I know the entirety of this article is false," he says, and turning from Adele, he walks away briskly.

"Well, that is good," she says to Cuori. "Let's go see your father."

Moments later, they find him leaning over the body of the pianoforte, intently focused on his work.

"Bart?" Adele says softly, unwilling to startle him.

He turns and on seeing her and his daughter, his eyes light up in the way Adele never tires of. "Hey!" he says, wiping dust off his hands on a rag.

"Hey," Adele says. She witnesses her somber tone quickly steal Bart's excitement. Before he can ask anything, she raises the paper. "You need to see this," she says and hands it to him. It is terrible to see his devastation as he reads, and when he looks up at her, she goes to him, wrapping him in her arms. Cuori joins them and all three stand together, united in their heartbreak.

CHAPTER
Twenty

Bart

*T*he warm glow from the flickering candle flame covers the dining table, where Bart sits surrounded by his small family. But what is usually a lively atmosphere through the dinner hour is uncomfortably silent. He eats the meal Adele has prepared but without tasting. Shame is bitter on his tongue. Until now, he has never in the last twenty-five years felt he couldn't take care of his family. To be called a fraud may not be the worst thing for some, but for Bart it is not only embarrassing but degrading. Who knew a single news article, based on an outsider's opinion, would make him question his worth or doubt his ability to be a good husband or father? And since when do dreams turn into nightmares?

He can still recall the excitement he carried when he and Adele first moved to Florence. It was an opportunity of a lifetime for him. He could put his first years as an instrument builder to good use even as he used his creativity to invent an instrument that could bring a world-renowned composer's vision to life. Now, that dream was shattered. The opportunity had ended in failure and the waste of thirteen years of hard work.

He finishes his dinner before Adele and Cuori, pushes his empty plate forward and rests his elbows on the table. He forces a smile at Cuori, his not-so-little girl. She sits like an angel, absorbing all the light in the room and then sending it back out through the brightness of her face. He thinks how like her mother she looks.

"What are you thinking about?" Adele breaks the silence.

Bart sighs. "What am I thinking about?" he responds, trying not to be sarcastic but failing miserably.

Adele has been supportive and kind all afternoon and evening, but when she replies, her tone is sharp, her posture rigid. "Yes. That is what I asked. Do you want to talk?"

"What is there to talk about?" he answers, keenly aware that he is pouting.

"I know you're angrier than you're letting on. You can tell me how you feel," Adele presses him.

He resents her pressing him. "I'm not angry."

"What are you then?"

"I'm sad. And I'm sorry. I'm so sorry."

"What are you so sorry about?" Adele inches her chair closer to him, but Bart can still hear an edge of annoyance in her voice. He feels Cuori's eyes watching him and knows she is paying her parents close attention. Ears listening closer.

"I moved us here for a job I was confident I could complete. I am obviously not capable, and the city realizes it now. I am an embarrassment to our family."

"That is the stupidest thing I've ever heard," Adele says softly, but without a trace of sympathy.

Bart looks up at her, brow furrowed. From the corner of his eye, he sees Cuori's mouth slightly ajar.

Looking back at his wife, he says, "I don't understand what you expect me to say then."

"I'm not going to sit here and pout with you. You have nothing to apologize for. You are a good husband and a good father. No one else's opinion could change that."

"But—"

Adele cuts him off. "And you are capable of finishing the job we came here for, maybe not in the time frame you first thought, but you *will* finish it."

Bart sits silently. The apparent tension in Adele's jaw tells him she isn't finished.

"And just because it's taking longer than you thought doesn't mean you are a fraud. This article was written by someone who doesn't fully understand the work you're doing. Their words mean nothing," she says with finality.

"Are you finished?" he asks respectfully.

"I am."

"I want to believe everything you just said. And it's probably true. But hearing someone say what I am doing is a waste of time and money confirms all my fears, and I am nearly convinced they are right."

"Why would you believe *one* negative opinion over countless positive ones?" Adele asks. "People believe in what you are doing, but now, one person has something bad to say, and you believe them?"

"I guess so."

"So, you disregard the support of the many people who know and love you but take hold of the one who wishes to use you as an engaging gossip topic?"

"No. Of course not," he says.

"Oh. So, you've just spent the last thirteen years patiently waiting for someone to confirm your self-doubt so you could believe it?"

"No. Not at all. I've worked hard on the pianoforte. I've developed completely new pieces of hardware, something no one else has done before. I don't just sit and brood over my shortcomings every day."

"Okay then, why are you letting this article bother you so much that you question yourself?"

"It's embarrassing for us—isn't it?"

"No, not really. Who cares what people think? What matters is what they know. And people who know us will see this for what it is. False. Just like Andy said."

"That is true." He knows in his heart that she's right. No one who really knows him, knows of the effort he has poured into creating the pianoforte so far, will believe the tripe that was printed about him. Bart rubs his eyes. "I'm just tired."

"Tired of what?" Adele asks.

"Tired of being encouraged then disappointed. Tired of being inspired then mentally empty. Between living and working, my life has been so up and down, and—" He pauses for a moment but then can only repeat himself. "I'm just tired."

"I understand. It's like a ship in the sea during a storm that never ends. Waves rising and falling. There is never a sunny day, only sunny moments."

"Exactly," he says, then dividing his glance, he looks from Adele to Cuori, his two sources of sunshine.

"Bart," Adele draws his attention, "we are on the ship with you." She gestures from herself to Cuori. "You're not traveling alone."

"I am so sorry, Adele. I'm self-absorbed."

"No, you're not. It is my responsibility to make my presence known. I have been a constant support, but I have failed to simply just walk beside you and validate your feelings. I'm the one who should be sorry."

He reaches for her hands. "You are the only reason I haven't given up one hundred times. You both are," he says. "You encourage me every day to keep going. I would not be where I am today without you."

Adele smiles. "I know, and I love being the one to support you, but sometimes the best form of encouragement is just being honest with yourself and the way that you feel. I never let you do that."

"It's okay. I love the way you motivate me; it is perfect."

"Good, but from this moment forward, I will remind you I am with you as we ride out the storm together."

"I would like that." He smiles, leaning in to kiss her.

"Eww. Gross. No kissing at the table, Papa!" Cuori shouts.

Adele and Bart laugh, and he feels the burden of his despair lighten. Countless times, being in the company of the two people he loves most, he finds a way to remove crippling fear and replace it with fresh hope.

"There is something else we need to talk about," Adele says.

Bart straightens on hearing the seriousness in her voice again. "What is wrong?" he asks, and following Adele's glance, he sees Cuori lower her head, watches as her shoulders sag.

Adele nods at her, but Cuori only squirms in her chair as if trying and failing to get comfortable. When she looks up at Bart, he sees that she is ready to burst into tears, and it tears at his heart.

Reaching an arm toward her, he pulls her chair next to his. "What is it, darling?"

She drops her tear-stained face, looking now at her feet, which no longer swing but touch the floor, and begins to tell a story that Bart doesn't believe at first, but as she continues, he realizes he might be naïver than a child.

CHAPTER
Twenty-one

1697 – Cuori
Two Years Later

*H*er auburn hair shows only tiny glimpses of what used to be striking blond strands. The hair on her head grows larger with each brushstroke. The static electricity crackles, matching the frequency of her anger. She looks at herself in the mirror, barely able to see her face through the frizz and flyaway hair. *I look ridiculous.* The thought isn't new. She likes the way her face looks when her hair is in a bun, not let down.

She is in her last year of school with only a few months of the school year remaining. In the previous two years, it has hardly been different for her. Still boring. Still easy. There is one thing new, though: her mother walks her there *every* morning, which means she can't explore the city and talk to Roald until she is inside the building and finds a way to escape unnoticed. Her stubborn and defiant nature has blossomed as she has matured into a teenager, but it is what has kept her friendship with Roald possible. Taking greater risks to see him.

"Are you almost ready, Cuori?" Her mother's voice, coming through her closed bedroom door, cuts into her thoughts.

"Yes, Mama," she responds disrespectfully.

"Then come to the kitchen and eat breakfast. And watch your attitude, miss. You don't want to press your luck with me today," Adele says.

Cuori hears her footsteps lead back into the kitchen and she mouths her mother's words, while she watches herself in the mirror. Maybe I do want to press my luck, she thinks, and getting up, she walks to her bookshelf, picks up a book she started last night, *On Motion*, written by a famous philosopher of Florence, Galileo Galilei, and then collapses on her bed to read. It's one of the first books he wrote. Roald recommended it to her, and she asked Andy if he had a copy to share, confident he did.

"Cuori?"

Cuori ignores her mother's call, and in a moment the bedroom door is thrust open. "So, you *do* want to press your luck?"

Cuori rolls her eyes so dramatically she can almost feel them grinding in her skull. She slowly closes her book and looks up in time to see her mother's hand as she grabs her ear.

"Ouch, Mama, that hurts!"

"Either walk with me to the kitchen, or I'll drag you there," her mother says.

"Okay, I'm sorry," she says, feeling at her mother's mercy.

When they enter the kitchen, she notices Sheila standing at the counter and her face burns, that she is being led by the ear.

"Good morning, Cuori," Sheila says, and Cuori's cheeks grow even hotter on seeing Sheila's effort to hide her smile.

"Hi, Sheila." Cuori tries for a nonchalant tone. She rubs her ear once her mother finally lets go.

"Grab a plate and eat before Anna and Luca get here so we can leave quickly."

"I don't want to eat," she complains. "Your food is gross."

Her mother glowers.

Sheila steps in. "Okay, then, why don't you come outside with me for a minute?" She looks to Cuori's mother, who nods, expression set in a long-suffering mode.

Cuori is certainly willing. Sheila isn't as annoying as her mother.

"What is wrong, little lady?" Sheila asks as soon as they have closed the back door.

Cuori turns her face to the morning sun. She breathes in the overwhelming smell of her mother's herbs. She loves the air out here, how it is invigorating, almost intoxicating. The sunlight glistens on the early morning dew, creating a vibrant landscape.

"Cuori?" Sheila prods.

She levels her glance. "I don't know what you mean."

"You know exactly. I know you love your mother, but how you acted just now is *not* love."

"She has become so annoying lately. I don't know, but she is," she says with a sigh.

"Do you think you're annoying to her too?"

"Probably," she admits.

"She has never said one unkind word about you or uttered one complaint. She cares for you and loves you, Cuori," Sheila says, elbowing her.

"Are you trying to make me feel bad?"

"No," Sheila says. "Walk with me." They begin walking through the rows of plants in the garden. The aroma of warm soil emanates throughout the garden. "I was your age once, and I remember what it was like for everyone and everything to feel overbearing."

"You remember that long ago?" she teases. "Just kidding!"

"Watch it. You'll be my age one day, too," Sheila says with a laugh. "As a young girl, it can be hard to manage all your emotions. Your body is still changing, and your mind must learn to process a lot of new feelings. Being short tempered is a side effect of that."

"I know all of this, but it isn't something I can control," she explains.

"No. You can't control what annoys you and all the other feelings, but you *can* control your attitude. Your mother is patient with you because she knows what it is like to be your age, too, but she is not patient when you're deliberately mean to her."

Cuori lowers her head and feels her cheeks flush red. "I don't try to be mean."

"But you are. You like your mother's food, but because you were upset that she pulled your ear, you wanted to offend her as revenge," Sheila says. "Am I right?"

"Yes, but she embarrassed me."

"Because I was there?" Sheila crows her neck. "I'm just an old lady."

"Still," she says, grasping for justification.

"Still, you tried to hurt her. Cuori, if you want your mother to respect you, then you will have to start respecting her. You're not much of a little girl anymore. Soon, you'll be done with school and getting married. You will need her in your life," Sheila says, hinting at experience. "You have what I didn't when growing up. Don't take it for granted and you'll save yourself a lifetime of heartache."

"I'm never getting married." She spits the words.

"When you meet the right boy, you will."

"It is hard to respect her when she tells me to do something I already know to do," she explains, wanting to change the subject back to the original one.

"She wouldn't need to tell you to do something if you would actually do it."

"I know what to do and I do it, just not in *her* timing," she says, her whole body growing hot from defending herself.

"Then do what you know to do in *her* timing. That is respect. She cooks for you, grows food for you, teaches you, and cares for you. Respect is the minimum you can do for her in return."

They begin walking back toward the house, and Cuori is tickled by the aromatic plants brushing her ankles as they pass, and she again breathes deeply of their scent.

"I can try." She starts to roll her eyes but stops herself. It has become a habit.

"Good. And if your impatience wins sometimes, don't let it stop you from trying again."

"Okay."

"Now, tell me you knew all that," Sheila says with a confident smirk. "You're a smart girl, but there is always something to be learned by those who have lived more life than you."

"I knew most of it," she jabs back at Sheila.

"Whatever. Just give me a hug."

Cuori walks back into the house and docilely sits down to eat the breakfast her mother has prepared. Not long after, when Anna and Luca arrive, Adele and Cuori meet them on the front porch and head toward the school.

Luca is as tall as an adult man, but his body has yet to fill out. When looking at him from the side, he almost disappears from sight. His slender build doesn't stop him from joining in on all the fights at school. He brings home a new bruise nearly every day, although his injuries are never anything serious. His personality is still gentle, and he is always kind and respectful to his mother and to Cuori.

She is more conscious of how she talks to Luca now. She can tell the way he looks at her has changed. The way all the boys in school look at her has changed. But then she has changed too, not that she is so comfortable with her almost fully developed breasts and the other changes in her body. Her mother and others tell her she's pretty, that her auburn waves rest against her glowing skin. They say the changes are why boys stare. All Cuori knows is that they make her a target for the most awkward conversations, Luca included. All the more reason, if she needed it, to flee school at the earliest opportunity.

Their morning walk ends at the school entrance, and, as usual, Luca sprints inside at the speed of light after saying goodbye to his mother. Cuori stops and turns to Adele. "I love you, Mama."

Adele steps forward and embraces her. "I love you even more."

"I'm sorry for this morning. I don't mean to hurt you."

Adele rubs the small of her back. "I forgive you. And I am sorry for embarrassing you. I never intend to do that."

She leaves her head against her mother's chest for a few moments more. The beat of Adele's heart is like the memory of a familiar and comforting song. The melody is still at the front of her mind. Adele kisses her forehead, and Cuori waves to her and Anna as she enters the building.

The tender moments shared with her mother aren't enough to keep her in school all day, and Cuori leaves before lunch, marching across the building to the east entrance that offers an unmatched view of the Duomo, which she admires a moment before jogging down the stairs and onto the side of the street heading toward a more preferred place than the school—downtown.

She has learned the network of streets in Florence better than the city employees themselves. Since the disastrous day she was caught by Andy, she has devised an efficient means of navigating the city—limiting the possibility of being caught again. The secret is using the position of the Chianti Mountains shadowing the city. She keeps them in her sight at all times, and they allow her to explore new areas without becoming lost.

The streets she has deemed unsafe in Florence are few and are all across the Arno River. The bridge connecting the city's two sides is her favorite place to stand and admire her home. The river divides the city into two parts, and the mountains on the right side cast a majestic blanket of shadow over the city.

Her fear of dangerous men has dissipated since the single circumstance two years ago now. She has learned that men who want to hurt girls are only interested in those who appear weak, so her gait and posture exude royal confidence. And it works because she hasn't had as much as a stare lasting more than a few seconds.

Every step she takes builds anticipation in her chest. *I can't wait to see Roald!* Her seventy-seven-year-old friend holds a special place in her heart, and his wisdom has a significant influence on her. He has been a stable friend, persistently kind and encouraging her to be herself over the last eight years. It is easier for her to listen to his advice than her parents, even though they say nearly all of the same things.

She arrives at the square, where the streets are always busy, and maneuvers around people until she stands on the corner where she always finds Roald. But he isn't in his usual spot. She can't find him either when she crosses to the opposite corner. Maybe he's lying down, she thinks, craning her neck in every direction. Quickly, she walks a small portion of each of the four streets where he might be, but with no luck.

Worry taps at her temples as she walks along the final street, but there is no trace of Roald anywhere. Where is he? He is always in this area, she thinks. Always. When she is in view of her favorite shop—where Roald buys her candy—she looks into an alley, and a familiar object, sitting in a trashcan, catches her eye. *No.* Denial pounds in her brain, but even as she walks up to it, her worst fear is confirmed. It is the painting of the field of wildflowers she made for Roald. She carefully pulls it out from the can piled with trash. It is unharmed, only covered in a film of dirt from years of living on the street with Roald.

She runs her fingers across it. Feeling the tiny and intricate brushstrokes sends waves of memories over her from the days spent painting it and the moment she gave it to Roald. That was the day she learned art was magic. The way his eyes burst with excitement and gratitude filled her heart with a sustained joy she can still feel. The moment became a part of her forever. *Why would he throw this away?* The question drifts through her mind. But her wonder is soon replaced by fear. *He wouldn't throw it away. Something is wrong.*

Tucking the painting under her arm, she runs back to the busy street, then slowing her pace she heads straight to the shop. If anyone knows where Roald is, it's Miss Loui.

"Hello, Cuori!" Miss Loui greets her from behind the counter, but her smile flattens as soon as Cuori shows her the painting.

"I found this in the trash. Do you know where Roald is?"

Miss Loui presses her lips together tightly and looks at the doorway. "I'm so sorry, Cuori." Her eyes become watery.

"What happened?" she asks with a trembling voice.

"Roald passed away two days ago."

Her breath is stolen from her lungs. Her heartbeat is so loud she can barely form a sound out of her mouth. "But I came to visit him two days ago in the morning. How..." She trails off. "Where did they take his body? I need to see him and put flowers on him, and his favorite candy, and his painting..." She stumbles over her words, which fall like a crumbling dam. When they can no longer be articulated, tears flood her face, and sobs pour out of her.

Miss Loui rushes around the counter and hugs her, embracing her tightly and shedding tears of her own. "The city workers took him the same day. I'm sure they've buried him by now," she says.

Grief is an entirely new feeling for Cuori, and she struggles to keep her balance, stay coherent, and not collapse under the weight of it. "Do you know what happened?"

"They assumed it was his heart. He fell asleep like usual but didn't wake up this time," Miss Loui recalls.

"It hurts so bad," she whimpers.

"I know. I know. You were his favorite person. He cared immensely for you."

What will I do now? Her sadness grows larger every moment she stands in Miss Loui's embrace. Finally, she lets go and immediately regrets it, feeling exposed.

"Do you want me to hang the painting on the wall? It would be our way of honoring him."

Cuori nods, then picks up the painting, which fell on the floor, and hands it to Miss Loui, but when she turns to find a place for it, Cuori rushes out of the shop. Her emotions were suffocating her inside the room.

The streets that used to feel warm and nostalgic now feel cold and depressing. The best part of the city is gone. More tears threaten her eyes, so she quickens her pace, trying to outrun them. She is jogging now, running toward the place where she can see the city and the mountains all in one view.

She stops before stepping onto the bridge over the Arno River and pants heavily. She leans forward with her hands on her knees to catch her breath. The city streets are still busy with horses and wagons carrying people and trade supplies. How can everyone carry on as if life is normal? She falls apart inside, while the city around her fails to miss even one beat.

After a while, feeling calmer, she walks onto the bridge that arches upward, and runs her hand along the stone edge. When she reaches the middle of the bridge—its highest point—she stops and looks out at the city. Her home. The late morning sun is high in the sky, reflecting intensely off the swift, rippling current below. The mountains in the distance stand tall and confident as they protect Florence. She has always wondered what it must look like here at sunrise or sunset. *I don't understand how he can be gone.*

She leans over the edge of the bridge, arms and heart hanging low. The calmness of the moment is quickly removed by the sound of shouting, signaling danger.

"Move, girl!" a man hollers. He leads a wagon carrying six barrels of wine, pulled by a team of four giant horses.

The wagon is nearly too big for the bridge, leaving no room as it passes by, so she quickly jumps onto the edge of the bridge, which is a couple of feet wide.

Steadying herself, she waits for the wagon to go by her. The coachman waves as he rides by. His previous shouting turned into a friendly grin. She does the same. When the wagon is gone, she pushes off the edge with both her feet to jump back onto the bridge. Instead of the push sending her forward, one of the stones breaks free from the concrete holding it in place, and it plummets into the river below. She feels her stomach drop and loses her balance. She collapses onto the stone-edge, her chest and ribcage taking the force of the fall. The sound of her ribs cracking floods her ears. Her feet dangle helplessly along the outside of the bridge, and her arms and hands cling desperately to whatever she can grasp. With all air knocked out of her lungs, when she cries out for help, nothing except a painful gasp escapes her mouth. Her weakening arms hold her up for only a moment before losing all their strength. When they do, she falls backward into the unforgiving currents of the river, unable to scream.

CHAPTER
Twenty-two

Adele

*T*he patio stirs with life as Adele and her two friends take a break from working in the garden and put the swing and rocking chairs to good use. They each sit holding a small glass of wine. Refreshing and rewarding. The bitter and sweet taste soaks their tongues and delights their taste buds. It's been an acquired taste for Adele, but after years of Anna telling her that dry wine is better than sweet, how could she not like it at this point?

Anna's knowledge of wine is no surprise, considering her husband is a winemaker, but her preference for dry wine is puzzling. Considering Anna's younger age and sweet personality, her liking of the bitterness of dry wine is a head-scratching topic.

"I have just always liked it, I guess," Anna says.

"Which is puzzling to me. I agree that it is better than sweet, but it wasn't until I was forty that I finally enjoyed it. Sweet was always my preference," Sheila says.

Adele raises her glass. "Sweet is still mine."

"Yeah, right. You should be used to the quality of dry wine now," Anna says.

"Just because I'm used to this bitter stuff doesn't mean I prefer it to the smooth and delicate," Adele admits.

"So, you never liked sweet wine?" Sheila asks Anna.

"I never had a chance to try it before I met Dario. As a wine-maker's son, he knew how much more of a story dry wine had to tell. The bitterness is time and experience, a delicacy to be appreciated. Sweet wine has no story to tell. Its only purpose is to please the taste buds for a moment."

"You sound like a winemaker's wife," Sheila huffs.

"I am. And I'm proud of it," she says, and they all laugh.

After a few silent moments, Adele looks up at Anna sitting on the swing. Her friend of fifteen years. And in that time, she has learned Anna is not good at hiding her emotions. She notices her subtle look of discouragement and sad eyes through her lingering laughter and half-smile.

"Anna, is everything alright today?" she asks.

Anna meets Adele's gaze, then glances at Sheila, who remains quiet but intently focused on her. She doesn't hesitate to speak honestly. "I spoke to Dario again last night. I told him that we have to move quickly if we want another baby. I'm thirty-five, and our son is a young man." She begins to stutter, visibly holding back tears. "But he became angry with me. He told me I was starting to annoy him."

Adele sets her glass of wine down and joins Anna on the swing. "I am so sorry, Anna."

"I guess I have enough of an answer now, though. He obviously doesn't want more children, even though he won't come out and say it," Anna says.

"I think you're right. He doesn't want more kids, but I am sure it's nothing you have done wrong," she consoles her.

Still nearly on the verge of tears, Anna says, "It's okay, I guess. Since Luca is grown, it would be like starting all over again."

"It definitely would be," Sheila says.

"I'm not sure I could handle being pregnant again anyway," Anna says, a smile growing on her face. "God, it was awful—worth it—but awful," she laughs.

Adele chuckles. "I was so glad to be pregnant past eight weeks. I hardly remember the pain, only the excitement of having a baby."

Anna and Sheila both remain quiet, studying Adele.

"It's too late for me now, and even if I could have another baby, I'm not sure I would be able to handle another teenage attitude," she adds, brightening her tone.

"Tell me about it," Anna says. "Trying to get Luca to do his chores is like pulling teeth."

Adele moves back to her own chair. "I wish getting Cuori to do her chores was the only issue. She is mean," she says, glancing at Sheila for validation.

Sheila nods her head. "That she is. But most teenage girls are."

"It really angers me though. She has no reason to behave the way she does. I don't know what happened to her, but she used to be an angel. It's like Satan got a hold of her and turned her into a demon." She laughs nervously. *That might be the issue.* She smiles inside at her bad joke. "That isn't funny, but it wouldn't surprise me at this point."

Anna laughs obnoxiously. "She is *still* your angel. She just doesn't show that side of herself much anymore."

"Never," she clarifies.

"It's because she is loved," Sheila says.

Adele and Anna both look at her, confused.

"She acts like a demon because she is loved?" Adele asks. "That makes no sense."

"When a child grows up in a safe and loving home, all of their emotions are let out freely. She feels safe to express herself as she learns how to control her behavior."

"I don't know..." Adele trails off with a doubtful tone.

"You said yourself that you fought and argued with your mother, right?"

"Yes," she admits.

"But not your father?"

"No. Never."

"You felt safe around your mother. You knew you were loved. But you didn't always feel that way with your father?" Sheila asks.

Adele shakes her head slowly. "I guess it makes sense. I was afraid of him and how he would respond to what I would say. I never was with my mother." *I trusted her. I knew she would love me no matter what.*

"I'm sure I was considered the perfect child. I hardly ever said anything and obeyed everything I was told," Sheila says.

"Does that mean you never felt loved by either parent?" Anna asks.

"I think I felt loved in some ways, but I never felt safe. Real love is safe. I never knew that growing up."

"I'm sorry, Sheila," Adele says.

Sheila acknowledges her with a slight nod and then continues. "My parents fought all the time, and I was often the reason. All I could ever think about was leaving. So, when I met a man who said he loved me, I saw a way out. He rescued me from my home, only to abandon me a few years later when I couldn't provide him with a child."

"That is so unfair," Anna says.

"Life isn't fair, sweetie. I've known and accepted that for most of my life now. But know, when a teenager lashes out, it's because they feel they are safe and loved and are learning how to control their response to the new emotions experienced at their age."

"Some days, it feels like she is just a spoiled brat. Bart and I probably should have disciplined her more."

"She doesn't seem spoiled to me. Spoiled children are disrespectful to everyone around them," Anna says. "Cuori is sweeter than pie to everybody except you and Bart," she says, holding back a small grin.

"I agree. If she is spoiled, she is spoiled with love and acceptance. This bad behavior will not last forever. Eventually, you two will be friends," Sheila says.

"That will be the day!" Adele says, throwing her head back and finishing her glass of wine. She notices a running figure approaching the house when she sets the glass back on the table beside the chair. She stands and squints her eyes. "Is that Luca?"

Anna quickly jumps to her feet and turns around to look. "It is!" she says, running past Adele and down the front porch steps.

Luca arrives at the front lawn, breathless. Anna meets him immediately, both speaking inaudibly, but even from a distance Adele can tell there is something wrong. She and Sheila exchange a worried glance. "Where is Cuori, I wonder," Adele says.

But now Anna and Luca approach, both of them somber.

"Where is Cuori?" Adele asks again.

Anna looks at Luca. "Tell her what you told me. It's alright."

Luca glances at his mother nervously, then begins spilling out words almost too fast to understand. "There was a group of men who came to the school. They worked for the city, I think, because they were all wearing the same kind of clothes." He stutters and pauses to refocus. "They said there was a body of a young girl found at the river's edge near one of the bridges. They came to the school to see if there were any students missing."

Adele's ears hear the words Luca speaks, but her mind is focused on only three: Body. Young. Girl.

Luca continues. "Two boys were missing from school, but only one girl. Cuori."

There it was—the name of her daughter. Confusion and panic explode inside her. "It is Cuori? Are you saying the young girl found at the river's edge is Cuori?" she asks in desperation.

"Nobody could find her, so I told Miss France she was not in the school, and one of the men said for you to go to the morgue across from the Duomo to identify the body. I ran here as soon as I found out," Luca finishes, and his voice breaking, he begins to cry. Hiding his face in his mother's chest, he says, "Do you think it is her, Mama?"

"I don't know, baby. I'm sure it's not, though. Don't worry," Anna comforts him.

"I have to go now," Adele says in a faint voice, stepping off the porch.

"I'm going with you," Sheila says. "You'll stay here and watch the house?" she asks Anna.

"Of course." Anna's voice catches.

Sheila jogs to catch up with Adele, who walks briskly.

What if it's her? No, it's not her. It can't be her. Adele's thoughts are a disjointed rattle in her mind. Her emotions are in turmoil, but the greatest of them is cold fear, underscored by a hotter current of confusion mixed with anger that Cuori had, again, skipped school.

"Adele," Sheila says, grabbing her hand, "be strong. Everything will be okay."

"How do you know?" she snaps but leaves her hand in Sheila's.

"It's all I know. Everything will be okay. We need to get to Bart without falling apart."

Adele nods her head, convincing herself what Sheila has said is true.

The music hall is a busy place on Fridays, especially during the middle of the day, and Adele and Sheila must thread their way through a crowd to reach Bart's shop. Before they enter it, a hand lands on Adele's shoulder. Wheeling, she sees Andy.

"Bart isn't here," he says somberly.

"Where did he go?" Adele is shaking and crosses her arms tightly around herself.

"He is on his way to the city morgue a block away. They found the body of—"

"A young girl. I know. That is why we are here."

"Yes." He gestures. "If you leave through the back exit there, you may catch him. He left only moments ago."

"Thank you," she says, and she and Sheila turn and walk quickly out the back of the building. "He knows something we don't," Adele says as they step onto the street.

"He is just worried for you and Bart, is all. But remember, everything will be okay," Sheila reaffirms.

Adele wants to believe Sheila, and she works hard not to assume the worst, but the adrenaline running through her veins is cold with panic.

The city morgue looms in front of them. The day is sunny and warm, but the building casts a dark and smothering shadow.

There are many steps leading to the entrance, but they surmount them in only a moment with long strides.

Upon entering, Adele sees a small desk to the right. A woman sits behind it with a kind face. "Can I help you?"

"My name is Adele Cristofori. I'm here to identify a body." Her heart pounds in her chest, echoing through her head and making it hard to speak.

"Her husband Bart has probably just arrived," Sheila says.

"I see, yes. It is the last door on the left." She points toward a hallway breaking off from the large entrance room.

"Thank you," Sheila says. They step away from the desk. "It's time for you to find Bart."

Adele jerks her head to look at Sheila. "You're not coming with me?"

"No. This is for you and Bart. You don't need me here."

"But you said everything would be okay," Adele says, voice beginning to fail her. Her knees threaten to give out almost sending her to the floor.

"And everything *will* be fine, Adele. Just go find Bart. I will see you soon. Alright?" Sheila says in a soothing voice.

Adele works at composing herself and nods. Sheila kisses her forehead and leaves her alone to walk into a room where she might find the end of her life as she knows it. *It's not her. It can't be her.* Denial cartwheels through Adele's brain.

Unlike the entrance, where sunlight fills the space, the hallway is not brightly lit. The candles flicker in the slight breeze she causes when walking by. Finally, she arrives at the last door and faces it.

If Bart hasn't come out yet, then... No. It's not her. Her mind argues with itself.

This moment and this place feel entirely unreal to her; her pounding heart is still the only thing she can hear clearly. Her breath remains fast and shallow. She pushes the door open and steps into a room even darker than the hallway. The only thing lit in the dark space is a body.

She recognizes every part of her daughter. Her feet and toes. Her fingers and hands. Her auburn hair and perfect cheekbones. Her forehead and nose dotted with a couple freckles like her father. She runs to her. She leans over Cuori's body and weeps. She screams with unimaginable pain.

Her body feels as if it will be ripped apart by the anger and sadness swirling inside of her like a deadly storm crushing her heart. When she falls to her knees, legs too weak to hold her, she notices the silhouette of her husband crumpled to the floor. His body shivers as he moans.

She falls in front of him, and he wraps his strong arms around her. They lament in the darkness below where their daughter lies, both unable to speak.

[Listen to 'Cuori']

CHAPTER
Twenty-three

Bart

*T*he aisle and pews of the Duomo are nearly filled with people making their way to the front to give their condolences. Only those with great influence in Florence and the surrounding cities are granted permission to hold a funeral at the cathedral. It was Andy who arranged it. Having known Cuori since she was an infant and being one of the most well-known and respected people in Florence, at his request, the Saturday afternoon spot was given to the Cristofori family without hesitation.

Bart and Adele both stand next to the open casket where their beautiful daughter lies cold. Tradition expects the grieving family to smile with gratitude for those attending the funeral in support, but neither is capable of doing so. Scattered throughout the long lines of mourners is the entire graduating class of Cuori's school, along with her teachers. Around thirty people. Bart's heart breaks for their sadness, but never more than when he sees Luca. His dark, shadowed eyes reveal the burden he carries for having been the messenger, bearing the tragic news of Cuori's fatal accident.

"I'm sorry," he mumbles into Adele's ear as he hugs her.

"It's okay, dear. We love you," Adele comforts.

He looks up at her, then quickly back down to the floor.

"You were her brother, Luca," Bart says, and pulling Luca into his embrace, he holds him tightly. "You are our family and always will be," he says sternly but with love. He feels the boy sag in his arms, feels his shoulders begin to shake with sobs.

"I miss her." He cries, and his tears dampen Bart's shirt. Still Bart doesn't let the boy go.

"I know," he murmurs. "We do, too." It is only with impossibly great effort that Bart maintains his composure.

But now, Luca breaks from Bart's grasp, and wiping away his tears, he turns and joins his classmates.

After students and teachers pass through, a single woman, unfamiliar to Bart approaches. "Do you know her?" he asks Adele.

She shakes her head.

"You two don't know me," the woman says, having must read their minds, and Bart sees her eyes are glassy with tears, "but I knew your daughter. My name is Chiara Loui. She would come to my store on Del Corso Street and buy candy often. I am so sorry for your loss. Cuori was such a beautiful child and brightened the room simply by being there. If there is anything I can do for you." She pauses to look at the crowd. "There probably isn't, but if by some chance there is, please let me know."

Clearly, the woman is one of the people Cuori went to see when she skipped school. Of course, Bart thinks, she would be a good person. "Thank you, Chiara. We appreciate that," he responds with gratitude.

Adele only forces a smile at her as she walks away. "Did she seem familiar to you?" she asks him quietly.

"Not to me," he answers. "But she seems kind." Adele doesn't respond, but he can't help but notice her desperate effort to place the woman.

After almost two hours, the lines of people eventually settle in the pews, filling about half the room. They prepare for the mass to begin. Bart and Adele find seats in the front row next to Anna and her family, Sheila, and Andy and his wife.

The priest, in a snow-white robe, arrives at the back of the stage area and slowly makes his way to the front podium, behind where Cuori's body lies.

Most of the priest's words bounce past Bart's ears. The entire day thus far has been a show of will, a matter of going through the motions. Exhaustion etches his mind, but he ignores it. No thoughts become concrete. Instead, everything feels fluid and indecipherable.

He holds Adele's hand, the only thing that still feels real, and together, they sit and wait for the priest to finish speaking about how God is good, and everything works according to His plan.

When the mass is finally over, the crowd begins filing out of the stunning and massive domed sanctuary. The front row, where Bart and Adele are seated with their friends, remains quiet. Bart is aware only of the shuffling of people exiting the building.

His attention falls on the many arrangements of flowers. The steps used to reach the altar are lined with bouquets. Adele brought a few of the paintings Cuori gifted to her over the years and placed them on easels across the altar. Bart can see and admire the detail in her brushstrokes even though he is several feet away, *if* he is even capable of admiring anything now.

As the nave empties, he grows nervous, and his palms clammy. Adele lets go of his hand. His right leg starts bouncing uncontrollably, and he leans forward to try and hold it still, only making him look all the more awkward and distressed. *I can't do this. I can't do this.*

"Are you okay?" Adele leans over to him and asks quietly.

Bart looks at her. Usually, kindness and respect flow out of him for Adele, but her question ignites an anger that has been waiting to be released. "Okay?" he asks, his tone dripping with bitter sarcasm. "I am *anything* but okay. How are you?"

Adele's eyes widen in shock, and then her expression contorts into embarrassment mixed with grief.

He wants to comfort her. To embrace her and tell her they will be fine. To be a strong husband for his wife. But he is not capable of doing anything except unleashing this anger burning inside of him, becoming more explosive by the second. "I have to go," he says with no emotion attached to his expression or tone.

Andy stands quickly when he hears Bart. "What can we do to help?"

Bart ignores his grieving wife and his friend and walks with long strides to the exit of the Duomo and outside into the grasp of a warm day.

The sun is still high enough in the sky to reach over the buildings, so he shields his eyes with his hand as he crosses a busy street and moves briskly to his shop with only one thing on his mind: the first concrete thought he has had today.

When he arrives at the music hall, he finds the main hallway dark and empty. He ambles along until his eyes adjust to the dim lighting and then quickens his pace again. Sunlight pours from the doorway leading into his shop. The large windows keep the room well-lit. *There it is.*

Immediately upon entering the room, his eyes land on the pianoforte. The object consuming the last fifteen years of his life. He approaches it slowly and runs his hand along its body. Every minuscule grain within the wood is sanded down to be perfectly smooth. The oil coating reflects the sunlight streaming in. It is an alluring piece of craftsmanship.

He walks around the gorgeous instrument so that now he stands at its front, where the keyboard sits. He peers over the instrument and glares at the action mechanism—the specific piece that has stymied him.

The fifty-four keys are each attached to their own padded hammer. The musician can play both soft and loud, but no more than a single note. The action does not yet have the ability to play a tune. When the hammer strikes the string, it immediately muffles the sound it produces. It is working out this defect that has consumed Bart for the last two years, yet no progress has been made.

The anger that fueled his abrupt exit from the cathedral has grown. The longer he looks at the piano, the more it rages within him. His unfinished work. The work he will be remembered for. The work that distracted him from his family. *His daughter.*

He inhales heavy breaths. Sweat begins rolling down his forehead. The beauty of the pianoforte no longer impresses him but mocks him. He looks across the room and locates a sledgehammer. He rushes to it, picks it up, and saunters back to the front of the pianoforte.

What am I doing?

He ignores the question and listens only to the urgent voice, telling him to strike. The room falls silent. His chest freezes. He lifts the hammer from the floor to over his head, then swings it with all his strength onto the keyboard.

Keys crack and fly apart, shooting them across the room like bullets. He swings again. This time, some of the hammers shatter, too. The strings echo the obliterating vibrations of the hammer. He swings a third time. A fourth. His anger releases a sudden and reckless energy into his veins, and his arms become like pistons, raising and lowering faster and stronger.

His mind is first on the instrument he is destroying but then on his daughter. With each destructive blow to the piano, he is slammed with the realization that he will never embrace Cuori again. Never look into her pure hazel-green eyes. Never see her smile when she is excited. The reality that his daughter is gone settles into him, adding more weight with every strike.

When he is nearly worn out from his effort, he thinks of his mother. The woman taken from him when he was only seven, his first love. The memory refuels his rage, and now, raising the sledge again, he goes for the legs of the piano, causing its cabinet to crash to the floor.

Pain consumes him. All regard for life is gone. There is only the voice of anger, and he is glad for it because it is the only thing holding him together.

Love led him here to this dark, cruel place. And love has a price he was not told about. It carries a grief too great to bear. He loved his mother with all his heart, yet she was stolen from him. He loved his daughter with every fiber of his being, yet the world also took her away. He never even had the chance to love the children he and Adele lost to miscarriage.

He screams now, and raising the hammer he brings it down unnumbered times, pounding the scattered pieces of the piano-forte, smashing them into smaller and smaller bits, and his cries echo throughout his shop and the entire music hall. At last, weak with exhaustion, he falls to his knees, arms stinging. But even his knees will not hold him, and he slumps onto his side, curling into a fetal position on the floor. Tears flood his eyes. The anger that acted as a dam melts away, and all that is left is his hollow, bottomless grief. He grasps his chest where his heart pulses heavily, and he weeps in both physical and mental agony until the slow darkness of sleep consumes him.

CHAPTER
Twenty-four

Bart
The Following Day

*C*uori stands on the bridge over the Arno River. She screams for help. Her voice is filled with terror. Bart notices her from the street below and tries to sprint to her, but his legs will only move in agonizingly slow motion as if he is walking through mud.

"I'm coming! Hold on!" he shouts to her.

She continues screaming, cutting a piece of his heart out with each cry. As he approaches the base of the bridge, he sees why fear is gripping her: the bridge is crumbling into the river. He begs his legs to move faster, but still, they move at a snail's pace.

Little of the bridge, where Cuori is standing, remains now. Her continued cries feel like enormous holes ripping in his chest. When she is finally almost within his arm's reach, the stone upon which she stands falls, and her body collapses into the river. Without hesitation, he tries to jump in after her, but his body won't listen. It is as if he is frozen to the edge of the collapsing bridge, forced to watch as his daughter is carried into the current of water and drowned. He screams at himself, "Move! Save her!" But his limbs don't obey.

The moment Cuori's lifeless form resurfaces, he bursts awake with bloodcurdling screams and spasms. When he realizes he is lying on the floor of his shop, his screams subside, and his body relaxes. Rolling onto his back, he lies still for a moment. He is aware of the pieces of oiled wood scattered around him, and the memory makes his heart sink like a broken ship. It is a while before he can sit up, and getting to his feet, he surveys the damage. The sunlight shining through the opposite windows from before he fell asleep tells him he stayed the entire night at the shop.

The legless body of the pianoforte is still intact, but only barely. He wipes a few beads of sweat from his forehead, then squats down in front of the remaining pieces of the keyboard. Most of the keys are broken, but he presses one of the few that are still intact. When he does, the hammer flies upward and strikes the string but immediately falls back. *It's broken.*

The same thing happens when he presses it again, except this time, he catches the sustained sound from the string even though he is still pressing the key.

He presses it a third time; the hammer flies upward and strikes the string but immediately falls back into its resting position, allowing the string to continue vibrating and producing sound, the sound which is usually muffled by the hammer and pressed key. He is intrigued but then discouraged as he realizes it is because the hammer is broken, and the key is now shattered from the damper—the piece that stops a note from ringing when not in use.

Straightening now, he again takes in the view of his fifteen years of work that lies in pieces around him. Why had he done it, destroyed it all? He can scarcely recall the rage that drove him. The only remnant of it is the anvil pounding against the walls of his head, and he digs his fingertips into his temples in an attempt to stop it. *I have to get out of here.* The urgency blazes across his mind.

He walks out of his shop and the music hall, and steps, blinking, into the bright sunshine. It occurs to him that no one would ever know what had happened to him if he were to leave and never return. He entertains the idea of vanishing as he traverses the city's streets. It isn't busy during early Sunday mornings, so he has the sidewalk almost entirely to himself.

After a few minutes' stroll, he arrives at the main bridge, which connects the two parts of Florence. He takes a deep breath and starts to walk across it. The morning sun is still low in the sky, casting his feet in shadow.

When he reaches the middle of the bridge, he stares at the space where the stone that should have held Cuori's foot should have been. It gapes at him, a black hole, drawing his attention. He feels pulled into its place. He swallows painfully, and he can't stop it when his mind replays his nightmare. The images come in ever more horrifying succession from the moment he learned Cuori had fallen into the river. He begins to cry. To weep.

"Why?" he whispers. "Why did the stone fall? Why did this happen?" he asks the wind. When it gives him no response, he yells, "Why!"

The pain of his reality grows too heavy for him. His knees threaten to buckle. He leans over the edge of the bridge and watches the current, letting it hypnotize him. The idea of falling becomes sweeter and sweeter until his entire body is lying on the edge— *just one more push.*

He tightens his muscles, readying himself to go over the edge. But suddenly, he feels a kiss from the wind on his face; it carries a familiar scent. Lavender. *Adele*, he thinks, and immediately the spell breaks.

He steps back. The river below is no longer mesmerizing but terrifying. He retreats several more steps, to the middle of the bridge, and rubs his eyes. He breathes heavily, trying to keep himself intact. His heart pounds in his chest, pushing adrenaline throughout his body. *What was I doing?*

Looking around him, he hopes nobody had noticed him there. Thankfully there are no tradesmen or canoes using the river early on Sunday mornings. When he has convinced himself nobody is watching, he walks off the bridge in the direction he came from, but with no destination in mind.

His steps carry him throughout almost every street in downtown Florence. Most shops are closed all day on Sunday, but some are open and busy. He avoids people as best he can, looking at the ground when he passes by someone. His somber face might draw too much attention, and he doesn't have the energy or desire to lift it.

The sun continues its ascent into the sky as he wanders the city, signaling noontime is arriving soon. His stomach begs for food, but he ignores it. He doesn't want to go home.

His eyes are on his footsteps, but his focus is on the pianoforte. Not because he destroyed it but because the broken hammer created the sustained sound he had been trying to achieve for years. How had it happened? He keeps asking himself, and slowly, different theories and testable ideas begin filling his imagination.

What if? The possibilities loom in his mind.

Every step seems to fuel his curiosity. He feels the twitch of desire. Where might it lead? Lifting his eyes, he takes stock of his location and, moments later, he is retracing a path to the music hall and his shop, where the pianoforte lies in pieces.

He arrives there quickly and with a subtle skip to his step. He finds the halls still dark, with the only light coming from the entrance of his shop. When he steps inside, he finds more than the pianoforte scattered on the floor: his wife is standing blank-faced in the midst of the wreckage.

"Oh," he stutters, surprised to see her. "Hi."

"Hi?" she scoffs. "Is that all you have to say after walking out on me yesterday and not coming home last night?"

"I'm sorry." He lowers his head, too embarrassed to meet his wife's eyes.

"Is this it?" She gestures to the pianoforte, what's left of it. "You've given up on your life's work? Are you going to give up on us too?" Her voice breaks on her tears.

Looking up into his wife's face, ravaged by grief, something breaks inside Bart's chest, and his face floods with tears, too. "I don't know." He shrugs.

"You don't know?"

"No."

Adele huffs with disbelief at the ceiling. "Okay. What does that mean?"

"I don't know—anything. My world is shattered. I'm sorry, Adele, but I can't be a good husband right now. I need to be by myself," he admits.

He can almost feel the heat rising up in her. "You think I know anything? I'm just as lost as you are, Bart, but I will always *try* to be a good wife. I am so sick of your pushover attitude. Every time something doesn't go your way, you want to give up." She laughs. "Look at what you've spent fifteen years working on, broken all over the floor. Look at us, twenty-seven years of marriage, and you are ready to give up. Why? Because life hates you? Well, life hates me just as much, and I'm not willing to give up." Her voice slips and catches. "I love you, and I need you right now." Her words heave and crack on her sobs. "You need me, too."

Stepping over pieces of broken pianoforte, Bart walks to her, and embraces her tightly, he whispers in her ear, "I love you too."

"I'm sorry for calling you a pushover. I didn't mean it," Adele mumbles.

"Don't apologize. I deserved it." He caresses the small of her back.

She takes a deep breath. "Let's go home."

Bart lets go of her and glances around the room. "I can't. Not yet."

"Why? I know it will be hard, but—"

"I need to stay here and clean up my mess. I need to be alone."

Adele steps back and huffs, "Seriously? Being apart from each other will not lead to anything good, Bart."

"Maybe. But I am serious."

She walks past him, purposely avoiding his eyes, but stops in the shop doorway.

"I love you, Adele," Bart says.

"If that is true, then you wouldn't abandon me," she says without turning to look at him. "I'll be at our home whenever you decide to join me."

Bart stares at the empty doorway for a moment after Adele leaves and then he finds a broom and dustpan and starts cleaning up the mess he made. He picks up what is left of the keyboard action and places it on the nearest table. He presses the key attached to the broken hammer, and the string sings. His eyes close and something deep inside him loosens. *I figured it out.* The thought rises on a quiet note of elation.

CHAPTER
Twenty-five

Bart
One Month Later

*T*he nutty aroma of tung oil circulates throughout Bart's wood-shop. The new body of the piano is far from complete, but its construction is well underway. He and Andy decided to shorten the instruments name since the approach to building it is now nothing the same. He coats the cut-to-length boards carefully and evenly with the rich oil, diligent to maintain balanced brushstrokes. He breathes softly and slowly to keep from stirring up excessive dust particles that cling to the wet surface and dull its shine.

Footsteps echo in the hallway, giving away Andy's arrival before he even enters the room. "Morning, Bart," he says, carrying a brown bag. "Brought you some breakfast."

"Thank you," he responds, not formally greeting him until he finishes the current brushstroke. When he finally turns toward Andy, his smile is forced.

"The piano will be even more beautiful than the pianoforte," Andy says as he admires the glossy and warm shine of the oil-coated pieces of lumber.

Bart chuckles. "Maybe on the outside, we will see how nice the sound ends up being."

"Speaking of sound, do you have the new hammer designed?"

"I do. Finished it last night," he says. "Want to see it?"

"Certainly!"

Bart glides to the other side of the room, Andy in his wake, and gesturing, he indicates the new hammer connected to a partially completed action mechanism sitting on top of a table.

"Pardon my first impression," Andy says. "But this looks exactly like the other one."

"It is. Except this one is broken."

"Broken?" Andy's expression is more curious than confused.

"According to how I thought the hammers were supposed to work, yes. But because the hammer is not fully connected to the key, it falls back from the string immediately after it strikes it." Bart presses one of the three keys to demonstrate. The sound reverberates across the room for as long as he presses the key. Once he lets go, the damper returns to its position and the tone fades.

"Wow!" Andy says, rubbing his forearms. "That gave me goosebumps. How does it work exactly?"

"I added this piece here." Bart points to a small, needle-shaped piece of wood connected to the many other moving parts of the piano. "I call it the escapement. When I press the key, it lets the hammer strike the string, but then immediately disconnect or 'escape' the key and fall away, which allows the string to produce sound until I let go."

Andy studies the escapement mechanism. "It looks like some-thing a surgeon would use. It's so complex."

Bart feels a rush of pride. "It is what we've been waiting a decade and a half for," he says.

"So, this is it? Now you just have to finish the body and the rest of the action mechanism?" Andy asks with excitement in his voice.

"Yes."

"My dream is all but a reality," Andy says, turning to look at Bart. "Because of you. This is absolutely amazing, Bart."

"Thank you, but it's not done yet. This one hammer took me an entire month to build. I'll get faster, but it will still take some time."

"We've waited this long; one or two more years is nothing," Andy laughs, and grasping Bart's shoulder, he clears his throat. "Our breakfast is getting cold. Let's eat."

Bart nods, and although he would prefer to eat alone, he fol-lows Andy back to the table near the door. Shoving aside a pile of lumber, Andy peels open his leather bag and pulls out a couple of linen-wrapped sandwiches and hands one to Bart.

"You've been here four weeks tomorrow," Andy says, after they've taken a few bites of their meal.

Bart nods, still chewing.

"When are you going to go home?"

Bart swallows. "I don't know."

"Don't take this harshly. I'm saying it because I'm your friend and care about you. You need to go home to your wife and stop hiding from your fear and pain," Andy says in his gentle and wise voice.

"You think I don't want to go home to Adele? I love her, but to go home is to accept my daughter is dead." He stops, and his body starts shaking. He looks at Andy with swollen eyes. "I can't."

Andy wraps an arm around him for a side hug as he says, "I do not understand your pain. I can only imagine. No one could ever blame you for thinking you can't accept it. But sometimes in life, we have to do what seems impossible."

"She was our little miracle," he says, and his throat narrows. His eyes fill. "She was my dream come true." He wipes his running nose on his shirtsleeve. "She made the world worth living in, and now..." He trails off, and for the first time in weeks sobs overtake him. He hasn't had to talk about it until now.

"It feels impossible." Without letting go of his friend, Andy finishes Bart's thought. "Impossible indeed," he repeats. "Do you think Adele feels the same?"

Bart nods.

"Yet, you two are having to handle it alone. Why?"

"I'm not a good husband. I'm too weak."

"It's not the husband's role to be strong all the time. Sometimes, we need to lean on our wives as much as they lean on us. Sometimes even more. Lean on Adele. She is much stronger than you realize. Let her carry you for a time. There is no shame in that."

"I just can't."

"But you must."

"I don't want to!" Bart yells, and Andy jerks his arm away, but Bart doesn't care if he's shocked. "I don't want to accept it. I don't want to move on or get better. I would rather this pain kill me."

"So, you choose to hide away from reality and eventually die from a broken heart?"

"I guess."

"Bart." Andy stands from the table. "I cannot make you do anything, but as a friend, I can't watch you self-destruct. You need to figure out what you are doing. Hide from reality all alone or face the impossible with countless people ready to support you, carry you even."

Bart stares at the floor and the silence that rises is unforgiving and hard. He feels Andy grasp his shoulder again.

"I'm here for you and always will be," he says, and then he is gone.

Bart wipes away his tears as he listens to the echo of Andy's footsteps.

I can't go home. The certainty feels carved onto the wall of his brain.

CHAPTER
Twenty-six

Adele

*T*he mid-morning sun beats down hot and heavy, and while it is still nothing like the relentless heat in summer, sweat beads on Adele's forehead, and her hair is soaked. Anna and Sheila work on rows to her left and right, harvesting bright red tomatoes and giant sweet peppers. The aroma of delectable spaghetti sauce will soon pervade Adele's home.

The warm soil beneath her toes and knees ground her with a sense of purpose as she stretches across the row of tomato and pepper plants. Any spears of grass or other uninvited plants are uprooted in her wake. The garden has always been her second home. In the last month, though, it has become her sanctuary.

Anna and Sheila are by her side every day. Sheila has stayed overnight since both Cuori and Bart no longer occupy their home, and Adele is alone. Anna comes over early and stays late. When Luca is not in school, he spends most of his time working with his father, as the Cristofori household is no longer a place of comfort for him. The same can be said for Adele.

As the three women work in the garden, it is mostly quiet, but sometimes conversations do arise. "Ouch!" Anna yells.

"What is it?" Adele asks blandly, assuming no real injury has occurred.

"That stupid weed was pokey." Anna and her flamboyant personality don't mix well with sweat and dirt beneath her nails.

"You should look at what you're grabbing first," Sheila smarts off.

"I did. Thank you," Anna says.

"Then why did you grab it?" Sheila asks, carrying on picking tomatoes.

"Because I didn't see the thorns on it," Anna whimpers, then looks up at the sky, shielding her eyes with her hand. "God, it's so hot." She wipes her face and leaves a smear of dirt.

Sheila stops and glances at Adele. "Looks like we are about to witness Anna's daily gardening show."

Adele laughs. "It's arriving a little early today, isn't it?"

"Shut up. I am not putting on a show. I don't understand *how* you two could possibly find this enjoyable," Anna says with emphasis on almost every word.

"What is there not to enjoy?" Adele asks.

"Oh, you're right. Who wouldn't love bleeding fingertips, dirty nails, a sweaty face and head of hair, and sore knees from crawling like a child?" Her voice rises higher and higher. "I'm not a child anymore, and my knees hurt!" Anna says, out of breath and on the verge of tears.

"There it is." Sheila laughs.

Adele can't stop herself from laughing, too.

"Shut up, Sheila! I hate you."

"I know you love me. It's just the garden speaking through you," Sheila says, chuckling.

"You know. That is so true. This is just not for me, but yet I still come out here with you both almost every day," Anna says with a philosophical tone now.

"Now, that is the definition of love," Adele says.

"Inconveniencing yourself to be with someone is one of the greatest expressions of love," Sheila adds.

"Much greater than just saying 'I love you,'" Adele says and rolls her eyes. Her mind jumps to Bart, and her initial anger softens almost at once into sadness that lingers only a moment.

Anna finds Adele's gaze. "As much as I love you, I am finished with this row, so I'm going to the house." Getting to her feet, she almost sprints to the shade of a tree beside the house where the tub of water sits.

Sheila and Adele finish weeding and harvesting their rows a moment later and follow behind Anna. They scrub their hands, wearily removing all the dirt beneath their nails.

"Let's snack on some tomatoes with basil and vinegar. I'm hungry," Anna says.

"Sounds good to me," Sheila says.

"We have that every day, though. You don't want to try something different?" Adele asks.

"Don't fix what isn't broken," Anna says, walking past Adele and Sheila and heading into the house.

Sheila shrugs in agreement.

In the kitchen, Adele pulls out plates, Sheila slices tomatoes, and Anna rolls basil leaves in her hand, unlocking the herb's powerful fragrance and taste. When the tomato slices are topped with basil and then drizzled with vinegar, the three satisfy their hunger cravings.

"Who would have thought just three ingredients could make for such a diverse mix of flavors exploding in your mouth?" Anna says with her mouth full. Her descriptions of taste are eloquent when she is hungry.

"I don't know, but it does hit the spot," Sheila says, walking into the living area; Adele and Anna follow her.

They silently finish their late-morning snack, and Sheila is the first to speak. "What is on the agenda for the rest of the day?"

Adele thinks a moment. "We can go to the market for a few things later if you want. Or who knows, maybe Bart will come home today." She laughs, and it is a grim sound.

Sheila and Anna don't join her. Adele notices they don't even smile.

Leaning forward, Anna says, "You have only ever made jokes about Bart's absence, Adele. How are you really doing?"

Averting her glance, Adele says, "I'm doing fine, I guess. I'm honestly not sure how I have survived this long without my baby girl and my husband." Her voice breaks, and she sets her jaw hard against the tears that want to come.

"You are the strongest woman I know," Anna says.

Adele meets Anna's glance. "I'm tired of being strong." And now the tears come, brimming her eyes.

Anna begins to cry too, and Sheila sits quietly, but Adele sees that her expression is soft with concern and love. She takes a ragged breath. "My heart is so broken, but I won't let it fall to pieces; if I do, I think it will stop beating."

"Let it fall apart," Sheila says, firmly.

Adele looks questioningly at her through a haze of tears.

"Whoever said you have to be so strong anyway?" Sheila says. "Let your heart fall to pieces. That's the only way it can begin to heal."

"But what if it doesn't?"

"Then you die, I guess."

Surprised by Sheila's response, Adele coughs and then laughs shortly on seeing Anna drop her jaw and glare at Sheila.

"She won't die, Anna. We won't let her, will we?"

"Never," Anna says. "I'm not good at puzzles, but I'll do my best to put your heart back together if I have to," she jokes.

Adele grins at her sweet friends. She clears her nose and throat. "Can you believe it has been a month?"

"It feels impossible," Sheila says.

Anna "Mmm-hmm"s, in agreement with Sheila.

"I keep waiting for her to come walking out of her room. I want to see her walking home from school with Luca or wearing one of her smiles. They were so adorable on her," Adele says. Fresh tears trail off her cheeks.

Anna scoots her chair close and takes Adele's hand.

"Why is she gone? Why would God give her to us and then take her away?" She swipes at her face. "How could this be a part of God's plan if He is *good*?"

"I don't know," Sheila admits.

"Nobody knows," Adele mumbles.

Anna straightens, then says quietly, "I don't think God has a plan."

Sheila and Adele both look at her. She doesn't need to be asked to explain herself. "When the priest said that 'God's plans are good,' I couldn't help but disagree."

"Because...?" Sheila says, letting her words hang in the air.

"Because God gives us free will. I think we so desperately want control but know it's not within us, so we convince ourselves that God has control and if we serve Him the right way, He will do what we want," Anna says.

Adele is surprised by Anna's conclusion, but it makes sense, she thinks. "So, then, what causes good things to happen instead of bad things and vice versa?" she asks.

"Life. We face the consequences of our own actions, but also those of the generations before us. They can be both good and bad," Anna answers her.

"If God isn't in control—with a plan—then why would you still love Him?" Sheila asks.

"I love Him because He loves me. Not for what I can get from Him," Anna says.

"I have never heard anything like that before," Sheila says, pondering Anna's words.

"I wish I could love God like that," Adele says. "I'm not sure I love Him at all anymore."

Anna squeezes Adele's hand. "And that's okay if you aren't sure. He will never stop loving you, though."

Adele cries again, and she is sick of it, she thinks. Sick unto death of her tears. She squeezes her friend's hand. "Thank you, Anna."

Anna hugs Adele and Sheila joins them, sharing their embrace.

"I'll always love you, too. Maybe even better than God," Sheila says, and when Anna pushes her shoulder, she yelps, "Ouch," and then smirks.

Adele thinks how their friendship has spanned more than a decade now. Perhaps it is the reason she has survived this month. Surviving the next one feels unlikely, but with Anna and Sheila by her side she might surprise herself.

"I have an idea for what we can do." she says.

Anna and Sheila both lean back into their chairs.

"Okay," Anna says excitedly.

"There was this woman who came to Cuori's funeral. I think her name was Chiara, maybe? Anyway, she said Cuori would come to her shop sometimes. I'm sure it was when she was skipping school. I'm just curious how well she knew my daughter."

"Her name is Chiara Loui," Sheila says confidently.

Adele looks at her. "Do you know her?"

Sheila closes her eyes and lets out a long exhale through her nose. "She is my older sister."

Anna's whole body jerks forward, as does Adele's. "You have a sister?" they both say in unison.

"Yes," Sheila says, then stands. "I can take you to her store."

"That is why she seemed familiar," Adele thinks out loud.

Adele and Anna quickly gather their satchels and follow Sheila out the door. Along the way to downtown Florence, Sheila tells them about her sister, and why she had never mentioned her before.

"We grew up in the same home, but she was ten years older than me. She was more my mother than my biological one was. She protected me from our parents and took a lot of their anger upon herself. That was until she found a man and moved out, leaving me in that house to fend for myself as a small child," Sheila says, no emotion tied to her voice.

"Oh no. That must have been when your parents' fighting started involving you," Anna says.

"Exactly. She left me in that hellhole, and never even looked back."

Adele catches subtle pain flicker across Sheila's face. "Were you angry at her?" she asks.

Sheila doesn't look at her. "What do you think?"

Anna and Adele glance at each other and cringe. Feeling sorry for Sheila, she asks, "Are you still angry at her?"

"No. I forgave her a long time ago. But I never wanted to have a relationship with her again. Still don't."

When they finally arrive at the storefront, a strong sense of familiarity rushes through Adele. *She was here.* She thinks of how Cuori must have spent many days along this exact street. She feels angry at her daughter's disobedience, but it is quickly replaced with longing to see her again.

She steps inside, holding the door for her friends, but when she looks back, Sheila is standing with her arms crossed, and Anna remains beside her.

"We will wait for you," Sheila says.

Slightly disappointed in her friends, she enters the store and approaches the counter. Chiara Loui has her back to her as she organizes some of the shelves of flour and spices.

"Hello," Adele says.

"I'll be right with you," Chiara says, finishing her task. Then she turns around and the softening of her face says she recognizes Adele. "Hi there. I'm so glad you finally stopped by."

$$\oint \flat \flat \, \, \text{🎹} \, \flat \flat \square$$

When evening arrives, the three of them unpack a small handful of pantry items from their stop by the market on their way home. The house is cool and dark until Adele dances her way around the kitchen and living area, lighting candles. Their glow brings a bit of warmth into the house.

Her heart is glad, feeling lighter than it has in the last month. Hearing the story of how her daughter impacted other people is such a gift. To know she was surrounded by people like Chiara, who seems so caring—enough even to hang one of Cuori's paintings in her store—and Roald, who apparently was like a grandfather to her before he died, brings a peace she can't describe. Still, moments of anger stir within her at the thought that if Cuori had obeyed and stayed at the school like she was supposed to then she would still be here. If she would have told her and Bart about the people she went to see then maybe they could have went with her to make sure she was always safe. Her mind fills with countless justifications of how her daughter should still be here.

As she leans over the dining table to light the final candle, she glances out the window and sees a familiar silhouette turning up the walkway. Light from the lowering sun is at his back, shadowing his face, but Adele can recognize her husband by how he walks.

"Bart is here," she whispers. Her heart sinks for some reason she doesn't quite understand.

"I didn't hear you," Anna says. "Who's here?"

"Bart." Adele lifts her voice over the sound of her pulse tapping rapidly in her ears.

"We're leaving now." Sheila takes Anna's hand.

Adele gives them each a quick hug and watches them greet Bart as they pass by him. Her conflicting emotions of surprise and anger gather immediately and with fire, ready to burn her husband alive if need be.

As he walks up the porch steps, she wants to stop him at the doorway and not let him through. She wants to tell him he waited too long and that she doesn't love him anymore. He hurt her too badly. Her heart races with each passing second, and then he is inside. She takes a breath to speak, but before she can Bart lifts his head and looks deep into her eyes. Her thoughts freeze. The fire inside turns against her and burns away all anger. Now she sees him

for the man he has always been. The man she loves. All she wants
is to run to him, but she doesn't move.

Bart stands frozen at the doorway. He doesn't break his eyes
away from hers, and when at last he takes a step toward her, she
can see he's trembling. His eyes start to glisten, too, in the flickering candlelight as if with tears. Her heart lurches in her chest at the
sight of his sorrow that so mirrors her own, and losing strength in
her legs, she begins to crumble. Bart sweeps forward and catches
her before she can fall and lifts her into his arms as if she were no
heavier than a summer breeze. Her sobs break on his chest.

Moments later as she quietens, he places her back on her feet,
but he doesn't let go. He holds her so tightly she worries her ribs
might break, but it feels good. She lets every muscle relax as her
tears soak Bart's shirt. She listens to his breath that, like hers, is
ragged with tears and to his heartbeat that seems to race in time
with hers.

Time passes, and eventually their shared grief grows quiet. Still,
they stand within the warm snug circle of their embrace. Neither
says a word for what feels like hours until she finally looks up and
into his eyes again. "You smell so good," she says.

Bart kisses her softly on the forehead. "I love you," he says.

"I love you too," she replies with a smile. Her whole body swells
with delight at being able to smile genuinely at the man she loves.
Her bitterness hid the truth from her. She wasn't angry at him. She
missed him.

"I'm sorry," he says. "I'm so, so, sorry—"

"Shhh." She cuts him off with a finger to his lips. "Not right
now." She takes a small step back that she might study his face but
remains close enough that she can still breathe in his scent.

He takes her hands in his, sniffing harshly. "I was scared. I didn't know what to do. I couldn't be strong." His voice cracks with every word.

"Bart, it's okay. You're here now, and we can figure everything out one piece at a time together," she says gently, and it pains her to see that his face seems to have gained a number of wrinkles over the last month. It is due to his bearing his sorrow all alone, she thinks.

"Have you been in—" He stops, looks away, then clearing his throat, he begins again. "Have you been in her—" But he can't finish, and his voice ends in a whimper.

"In her room?" Adele knows what he is asking.

He nods and wipes his face.

"No. I haven't."

He inhales deeply, drawing in a chest full of air, then exhales gustily.

"Do you want to go now?" she asks.

"No," he answers. "In the morning."

[Listen to 'Reunited']

CHAPTER
Twenty-seven

Adele
The Next Day

*T*he sound of breathing wakes her from the deepest sleep she has had in recent memory. When she rolls over and sees the back of Bart's head, she is at first confused. The month apart felt like a lifetime. *At least Bart is home now. I'm not alone.*

Adele probably would have punched him if it had not been a surprise when he came home last night. When he moved toward her, though, any desire to hurt him left her mind, the same as now, watching his chest rise and fall from steady and deep breaths.

"I've missed you, Bart. I love you," she whispers, and she scoots closer to him, running her fingers through his hair and massaging his scalp. Even in the intricate and tiny blood vessels on the top of his head, she can feel his heartbeat, a gift her daughter gave to her. She fights back the urge to cry as she is overcome with gratitude to

have him back and to finally be next to him again. A broken heart
cannot heal alone.

When her touch finally wakes him, he rolls over to face her.
"Good morning, my love," he says, ending with a yawn.

"Good morning. Did you sleep well?" she asks, with a smile that
feels sincere for the first time in a month.

"So good," he says, then looks across the room as if collecting his thoughts. "First time I didn't wake up from nightmares in a
while." His eyes return to hers.

"You've had nightmares?" she asks with empathy.

He nods.

Her heart feels his pain. "I'm so sorry. I should have come to
see you instead of staying away."

Bart's expression changes to one of confusion. "Please do not
apologize. I asked to be alone, which was stupid, and I see it now. I
will be asking for your forgiveness for the rest of our lives because
I left you, and I understand if you never forgive me."

She puts her hand over his heart. "I've already forgiven you.
You don't need to ask anymore."

Bart kisses her on the forehead, then her lips. "I love you so
much," he says, then wraps his arms around her and pulls her close.
His touch brings reassurance, burning away any remaining doubt
about his love for her.

"Are you ready?" she asks.

His gaze becomes solemn and cold. For a moment, he is silent,
and she is afraid she has upset him, but then he says, "No, but
it's time."

They both rise. Adele dons her gown and Bart pulls on his robe.
What they are about to do next makes leaving the comfort of their
sheets all the more difficult.

Cuori's bedroom door has remained shut since the day she left for school and didn't come back. The air inside will undoubtedly be stale.

Bart and Adele stand outside Cuori's bedroom, contemplating their decision to enter today instead of waiting for a day when it will be easier. Which they both know would never come.

Bart leans his head against the door. "A part of me is hoping that when we go in, we will find her lying in bed reading or sitting on her stool chair painting."

Adele intertwines her arms around his waist. *All of me is hoping for that.*

After a few moments of standing at the door, Bart reaches for the doorknob, twists it, and pushes it open.

Adele immediately bursts into tears. The overwhelming aroma that defined her daughter floods her nostrils—minerals with earthy sub-notes from the paint. Vanilla and wood from the pages of books, one still splayed upon her bed. The room is not stale but full of life. Even the fragrance emanating from the sheets is not musky but sweet like their daughter always was.

Adele collapses on the floor, the memories becoming too heavy to carry. She covers her eyes with her hands until she can collect herself. *My baby.* The words sear her brain.

Above her, Bart is still standing, but she hears him weeping. He grips his chest and bawls as he gazes around the room. Her colorfully painted shoes are by the door, and he has to step over them upon entering. The countless paintings on the wall. The paintbrushes. The small cup of water still sitting on her table to dip the brushes in is murky with pink clouds. The unfinished painting sitting on her easel is of a sunset over the Chianti Mountains.

He stumbles to her bed and falls without grace onto it. He pulls his knees to his chest and lets his tear ducts empty themselves.

When Adele has regained a degree of composure, she uncovers her face. The aroma's still overwhelming, but now she can at least see Cuori's belongings. Remaining on her knees, her glance takes in the chair where Cuori would sit to comb her hair. It is close enough that Adele can see strands of auburn-colored hair. They glint in the morning sunshine like little pieces of gold. Rising, Adele scoops them up in her hands and holds them to her chest. Then she picks up one of Cuori's shoes and, lying on the floor on her side, she holds to herself the remnants of her daughter that she has gathered. She is helpless to stop her heart from falling apart, although she knows the risk is that it will never be put back together.

CHAPTER
Twenty-eight

1699 – Adele
Two Years Later – September

*I*n autumn, the weather in Florence is crisp in the mornings but warm by midday. Pleasant is how Adele would describe it. She sits on her front porch in a wooden rocking chair, watching the sunrise above the city stretching out in front of her. A gentle breeze whips a few strands of hair across her face, and she pulls them back behind her ear. The gray at the roots of her glowing blond hair is the only evidence of her grief-stricken heart. Her face remains unlined, unlike Bart's; he has aged ten years in twenty-four months. His hair, skin, and posture all reveal the stress he has undergone since Cuori was taken from them.

Adele looks around at Bart when he emerges from the house, carrying his bag containing the lunch that she prepared for him earlier. She feels his lips stir her hair when he leans down to kiss the top of her head, and she watches him as he steps off the porch until he disappears from her view.

The two barely speak to each other these days, and they never talk about Cuori. Bart has been burying himself in the work of finishing the piano over the last two years and comes home exhausted. Adele spends her days in the garden and with Anna and Sheila. It would seem to an outsider that she and Bart don't really need each other. That they love one another is unquestionable, but their relationship has deteriorated.

Adele is happy for her husband. He has spent seventeen years now on the piano, and according to what he last told her, he is almost finished. All that is lacking, he says, is the addition of a few more aesthetic pieces to complete the instrument's unique look. Without these final touches, he claims that in appearance the piano would be inseparable from the harpsichord.

She tries to visit him at his shop at least once a week but has missed going there this week and the last. He doesn't acknowledge her arrival or her presence but continues working as if she isn't there, making her feel unwelcome and out of place. In fact, she would have no one to talk to when she goes to the music hall other than Andy and, on occasion, Frank. But Frank is on the opposite side of the massive building, so she doesn't see him unless she makes a specific effort.

She closes her eyes now. *Lord, let him have a good day.* As the prayer takes form in her mind, it is quickly interrupted by voices mixed with laughter coming from the street. Anna and Sheila, Adele thinks, and her heart gladdens. She is so grateful for them and their loyalty. Anna no longer brings Luca. He has been finished with school for over a year and is a full-grown man now, working with his father at the vineyard. Dario and Anna are discussing buying the business in phases over the next few years from its current owners, a wealthy husband and wife with no children to inherit their business. It is a huge financial opportunity for them and something they are immensely proud of.

"Good morning, beautiful!" Anna says. Sitting in the chair next to Adele, she lets go a dramatic sigh as if her morning walk took all her energy.

Sitting across from Adele, Sheila peers intently at her and says with her usual perception, "You look like you've been thinking a lot."

Adele lifts her brows. "What gives you that impression?"

"Your hair has so much static in it. I'm assuming it's from all the work your brain has been doing," Sheila chuckles.

Adele runs her hands along her hair. "It's these humid mornings."

"So, you weren't thinking about anything?" Sheila asks.

"Well, yes," she admits. "There isn't a moment I'm not thinking. Mostly unimportant things."

"Then I like my reason for your staticky hair more than the humidity in the air," Sheila says.

Anna joins in, laughing as she says, "I get that, I never stop thinking either."

"Andy has let me bring home and read some of Cuori's favorite books. Now, I think even more, but about philosophical things. No wonder she was so smart. Those books are complex even for me," Adele says, smiling at the thought of her daughter's intelligence. "She was especially interested in Galileo Galilei. The way he saw the world and connected it to the universe is magical."

"Yeah. She could've outsmarted all three of us," Anna says.

"No doubt," Sheila agrees.

An awkward silence falls. Anna quickly ends it. "How was Bart this morning?"

"The same," she says, sounding defeated.

"I'm sorry," Anna comforts, tipping her head against Adele's shoulder.

"I wish he would come home with a smile and whistling a tune like he used to. But he is completely different. Everything is, though, so what does it matter?" She shrugs.

"It matters," Sheila says. "Longing for the person you love to be happy again is not a vain wish."

Adele looks gratefully at Sheila.

"You two still don't talk much?" Anna asks.

"Hardly at all. What's necessary or from habit. We say, 'I love you,' 'good morning,' and 'good night.' No words to help anything."

Anna leans back in her chair.

Sheila notices Anna's withdrawal, then says, "At least you say that much. It's better than nothing at all."

Adele rolls her eyes. "It's like living on scraps."

"Hey, I've been there before. There is no shame in living on what you can to survive. Even if it is begging for scraps."

Adele feels childish for complaining. "I'm sorry. You're absolutely right. It could always be worse. I guess I should lower my expectations for now."

"No. Don't do that. Always keep high hopes but be patient. I can't speak for you or Bart, but with how much you two obviously love each other, this is bound to work itself out eventually," Sheila says.

She nods. "Thank you for that, Sheila. I don't know what I would do without you."

"If a person like her," Sheila points to Anna, "was all you had, *then* you'd be in trouble." She laughs.

Anna looks at Adele and coolly says, "She is probably right; everyone needs at least one bitch in their lives."

Adele drops her jaw, feeling scandalized and then bursting into laughter.

"No offense," Anna says to Sheila, trying but failing to prevent her guilty smile.

"None taken," Sheila says, and all three share a giggle.

"Oh," Adele sighs. "I needed that laugh."

"If we are good for anything, it would be that," Sheila says.

"What would be the point of living if there were no laughter?" Anna asks, not expecting an answer.

"No point at all," Adele says. "There are too many bad things in the world as it is. The little bits of joy we find are the only way to endure them."

"That is so true. I want to always be a bit of joy!" Anna shouts.

"You are more than a bit." Adele turns to look at Anna. "You are a mountain of joy."

Anna takes Adele's gaze to her heart, and tears fill her eyes. "That is the most precious thing I've ever been told." She stands and leans onto Adele to hug her.

Even Sheila, who is always unflappable, Adele thinks, has to wipe away a few tears of her own.

"Get in here, Sheila." Anna stretches out her arm.

Sheila joins in the hug, and the three of them laugh and cry together, embracing the definition of a true friendship. "I love our hugs," Sheila sniffles.

"Okay, enough time crying. Let's go to the garden," Adele says.

"Oh great. This mountain is about to turn into a valley," Anna whines.

"At least it isn't hot anymore," Adele says.

"That is true," Anna says.

"She will probably still complain," Sheila jokes.

"That's true too," Anna admits as they walk around the house
to Florence's most beautiful and intricate garden.

CHAPTER
Twenty-nine

Bart
1699 – October

*T*uning the piano isn't all that different from a harpsichord. He shifts his attention to the final three strings, twisting the bolt with minuscule movements so as to not break the fragile string—which he has done many times. He is guilty of learning some things the hard way.

This is it, he thinks as he finishes tuning the last string. *It's actually finished.*

The realization of his work finally being complete has yet to settle on him. After spending seventeen years building a single instrument, it has become an enormous part of his life. Now that it is over, he feels like it went by fast. *It feels like it has been forever, but also like we just moved to Florence.*

The time spent building the piano included the best and worst parts of his life—the birth of his daughter and her death. Two years have passed since Cuori left, and still, there are days when he thinks he will see her on his arrival home in the evening; instead he is cruelly reminded of her absence.

He has been so busy with finishing the piano his grief has had little time to process. The grief of losing Cuori hasn't affected his work but has separated him from Adele, the woman he loves more than life itself. And although he loves Adele, it has been hard to be intimate with her. Her presence is an overwhelming reminder of Cuori. He feels like a stranger in his own home, and all he can think about when he is there is leaving.

He has a solution in the works, though—an idea to fix their relationship has been forming over the last couple of weeks. And he has enlisted help.

Footsteps outside his shop in the hallway interrupt his thoughts, announcing he has a visitor. He can tell by the pace that it's Anna. *Perfect! She is on time.*

She walks in with her typical energy today. Bart has often thought it's as if her smile and joy is brighter than the sun itself. Her hair is long and brown, a shade of auburn that is like Cuori's. It is the same shade his hair is. Sometimes, he wonders if Cuori would have looked similar to Anna had she lived to become a woman.

"Okay, here is the plan," she says excitedly, wasting no time with greetings.

"Let me hear it," he says, folding his arms.

"You will go home, bring her here..." She trails off when Andy walks into the room.

"Hello, Anna! How is a fine lady like yourself doing this lovely day?" he asks, placing his hand gently on her back.

"I am excellent. I was explaining how this afternoon needs to go to set up the trip for Bart and Adele," she says.

"Perfect, how can I help?" he offers, and he listens as Anna details the events of the upcoming hours.

Now that the piano is complete, the original plan was to unveil it to the media and all of Italy in November, but last week, Bart had asked Andy if they could wait until the first Saturday of the new year.

"We have waited seventeen years for this moment. What is another two months?" Andy had said. "But can I ask why you want to postpone it?"

"Adele," Bart had said.

Andy didn't respond. He had only looked at Bart and waited for him to continue.

"We've grown apart since we lost Cuori. I've been a terrible husband and focused on the piano instead of her. Now, I want to put her first. Like I should have done the whole time."

"For just two months?" Andy had asked with a smile.

"I have a trip planned. It will take two months."

"Sounds like a beautiful idea. Please take it. We can wait for the new year to unveil the piano. Besides, an extra month to practice my compositions on it is probably a good idea anyway. I'm not as young as I used to be, and it takes me longer to memorize now."

"Thank you, Andy," Bart had said.

"Bart," Anna says, bringing his attention back to the present day.

"Sorry. I'm still listening," he says.

Anna talks fast as she wraps up the schedule for Bart to go home around lunchtime and bring Adele back to the music hall while she and Sheila pack Bart and Adele's clothes into their trunks. "Act casual. She won't be surprised if you give it away with your body language."

"I think she will be surprised no matter what happens," Bart says.

"It sounds like I just need to stay out of the way?" Andy asks.

"Yes. Until Bart and Adele come out of the music hall to get into the carriage, you need to be out there with all of us to give them a big farewell."

Andy raises his brows. "Got it."

"I am so excited, and I'm not even the one going on the trip!" Anna says.

"Thank you for your help with this, Anna. I couldn't have done it without you," Bart says.

"My pleasure! I hope you use some of my ideas," she says with a grin.

The three of them disperse, and Bart puts away his tools for the day and then picks up other clutter and stores it. Before he leaves, he stops in the doorway to look behind him. The clean and tidy shop allows the piano to shimmer like gold in the middle of the room. The fresh coating of oil magnifies the grains of the cypress wood. *It's actually finished. I finished it, Cuori!*

He takes a deep breath when he arrives at the front of his home at midday. Two years of emotional separation cannot be fixed in a moment, and he knows that, of course, but a huge part of him is hoping it can. Fixing a relationship is also not easy, yet the entirety of him hopes it will be. *This is it.*

He steps onto the porch, pushes the front door open, and walks inside. Sheila, Anna, and Adele are sitting in the front room, laughing, until Adele turns around and sees him. The room grows silent, but not for long.

"Bart! It's so good to see you. Been awhile," Anna says as she walks to him and gives him a hug.

"Likewise!" he responds, trying not to appear nervous.

"Come on, Sheila, let's give them some privacy."

"Hi, Bart." Sheila stands, her face a knot of confusion. Bart knows from Anna that she didn't confide in Sheila.

"What are you doing here this time of day?" Adele asks as Sheila follows Anna outside.

Bart thinks how the physical distance between them is less than five feet, but it feels more like oceans separate them. "Adele."

She stands to face him as he speaks her name.

He can't think for a moment and studies the floor. But then, composing himself, he looks into her alluring eyes. "I have so much I want to say. I couldn't possibly say it in one sitting, so will you walk with me? I want to take you somewhere special. Special to both of us." His voice is shaky at first but more poised at the end.

She huffs air through her nose, then grins. "Sure."

His face lights up, and it's just now he realizes he was afraid she would say no. "Perfect! Let's go." He walks back to the door and holds it open for her.

"Maybe I'm just better at keeping secrets than you thought." Anna's voice rings through the open doorway.

Bart cringes.

"Shhh," Sheila says.

"What are you two discussing?" Adele asks them, curious.

"Nothing important. Bye." Anna maneuvers around Adele and Bart, stepping back inside the house. She pulls Sheila along behind her and quickly closes the door.

"That was strange," Adele says, squinting at the closed door.

"They're your friends," he says with a shrug.

Adele glares at him, then punches his shoulder and smirks.

"Ouch, what was that for?" Bart laughs, rubbing his arm.

"Only I can make jokes about my weird friends," she says, trying to be serious, but is betrayed by a sudden burst of laughter. "Anna is awful at keeping secrets. She has to be a part of whatever is going on." She looks at Bart for confirmation. "Well?"

"She might have helped me in *some* ways."

"What is going on? Where are we going?"

"Hey. No questions. This is something for you, and I want you to be surprised."

"A good surprise?" she asks.

He hesitates.

"Bart!" she yells at him.

He smiles from ear to ear. "Yes, my love. A good surprise." His heart begins to swell, or at least his chest warms. He had forgotten how much fun Adele is to talk to. Her confident personality always pulls out his favorite parts of his own. He is the most authentic version of himself when he is with her. *This trip will be like getting to know her all over again.*

They arrive near the music hall in less than an hour. The city streets are becoming busier, with it being an early afternoon on a Friday. A clearing finally opens in the street, and they dart across and enter the building.

"Why are we here?" Adele asks, then she gasps. "You finished the piano?"

"Actually, yes. But that's not why we are here."

Adele's jaw drops and she stops walking. "You finished it?"

"Yes."

"Can I see it?"

Bart exhales. "Yes, really quickly. I brought you here for something else."

They walk along the dim hallway to the other side of the music hall where his shop sits. When they come to the entrance of his shop, he lets her walk in first.

She takes a few paces into the room, then stops and covers her mouth. "Oh my."

He arrives at her side and notices the tears streaming down her face. "Why are you crying?" he asks and wraps an arm around her. She rests her head on his shoulder.

"It's gorgeous."

With the afternoon sun still high in the sky, the light coming in the windows is not direct, which gives the room an elegant ambiance. The piano's grand size, unique colors, and majestic presence fascinate Bart's eyes, and clearly Adele's too.

"You did it." She lifts her head to look at him now. "You did it!"

His eyes get lost in hers, and he is tempted to cry too but reminds himself to save his tears for what he has planned.

"What does it sound like?" she asks.

"Not now. I'll let Andy show you. He has already written multiple songs."

"Seriously? I don't get to hear it?" she whines.

"Not today."

"Fine," she says, but Bart feels her disappointment and takes her hand, leading her from the shop into the hallway. He slows their pace as they near the auditorium, and still holding her hand, he asks, "Adele, it's been a long time, but do you remember the tune Frank and I played for you on your birthday nearly ten years ago?"

She smiles at him. "I could never forget."

"Good. Because I'm going to play it for you again," he says excitedly.

Her eyes widen. "Really?"

"Yes," he says, then pulls her into the auditorium, where Frank sits on the stage beside his violin.

"Good evening, Adele. You look beautiful as always," Frank says, bowing slightly to acknowledge her.

Adele stares at Bart with a growing smile. *She is already speechless!*

Bart helps her onto the stage and gives her a chair facing Frank and himself. As he reaches for the guitar and sits down with it in his arms, he says, "This tune is many years old now, but it is an expression of my love for you that still remains, even though I've been bad at showing it." He almost chokes on the last few words.

Adele's expression softens with a tenderness Bart hasn't seen in her since before they lost Cuori. Is there hope for them still? Only time will tell. All he knows for sure in this moment is that here and now, in the soft light of flickering candlelight, she looks to him like an angel.

"I might not make it through without crying," he tells her. "A lot. But I'll do my best to keep playing," he adds with a chuckle. He exchanges a smile with Frank and when he finally feels ready, he strums the first chord of the tune. Frank grins at him, then Adele, and waits.

The music hall is the epitome of good acoustics, and when the guitar strings vibrate against the wood, the vast room bursts to life with vibrant and warm sound. Bart is grateful when Frank allows him to play the first full chord progression before he comes in with the violin. When he does, Bart feels the melody rip the room in half, with reality on one side and heaven on the other, and they each sit on the side of heaven.

The melody expands, becoming more dynamic. Bart plays faster, adding more chords to fill any empty spaces. His mind, the very room, takes on an utterly ethereal feel until Bart finishes the tune with one last gentle and soothing chord progression that flows like a lullaby.

The room becomes silent. Bart seeks Adele's glance and finds she is a mess, wiping tears from her eyes and sniffling. Finding his own face wet, he uses his shirtsleeve to wipe away his tears. Frank divides his smile between them, and Bart knows he is happy to witness and to participate in such an expression of love. A moment later, Frank sets down his violin and steps off the stage, leaving the room.

Bart puts the guitar aside and approaches Adele, offering her his hand, and raising her from her chair, he embraces her. She rests her head on his shoulder, and his strong arms enfold her as the silence around them is disrupted only by Adele's sniffling.

"I love you so much, Adele." Bart breaks their silence. "I hope you can forgive me for the pitiful husband I have been."

Adele pushes off his chest to look him boldly in the eyes. "I have been an equally pitiful wife."

Bart smiles at her. *She is perfect in every way. How could she think she has been a pitiful wife?* "I have a trip planned for us, and I'm hoping it can restore us, fixing our relationship. If you want that too?" he asks her.

Adele continues to gaze at him, speaking volumes with no words. "No. I don't."

His heart pauses and he feels a weight of fear mixed with anguish.

"Bart. We can never be restored. We are broken beyond repair and can never be *fixed.*"

"But—" he tries to cut in.

"Restoring our relationship means going back to how we used to be. We can't. Cuori is gone. Trying to go back is futile. We don't need restoration. We need to fall in love with each other again.

We need to learn all the new parts of one another where grief has changed us. We need to grow back together, not the same, but even stronger than before. Otherwise, we will never survive." She takes a deep breath. "I don't know what the word is, but I know it isn't restoration or fixing." Adele's voice is passionate, and in it Bart hears the echo of his own desperation that has built up over the last two years.

"Healing." He supplies the word.

Adele closes her eyes. "Yes," she whispers. "We need to heal."

"So then, my incredibly gorgeous and lovely wife, Adele, will you go on a journey of *healing* with me?" he asks whimsically, putting a strand of her hair that had fallen across her face behind her ear.

She smiles brightly at him, eyes welling up again. "Yes, my remarkably handsome and incredibly talented husband, I will," she giggles.

His heartbeat quickens, and it's pounding like a drum of joy. *Here we go!*

"Follow me," he says, taking her hand and walking quickly out of the music hall and onto the street outside where the carriage and coachman are waiting.

When they exit the building, they find not only the carriage but also Andy and his wife, Frank and his wife, Sheila, Anna, Dario, and Luca. They all stand in a rainbow-like line and watch as Adele and Bart approach.

Adele's face exposes both a quick onset of excitement and confusion. She glances at Bart. "What is this?" She notices their trunks in the carriage. "Who put our stuff in there? We never ride in a carriage," Adele points out.

"That would be Sheila and I," Anna says, smirking. Proud of her well-executed mischief.

"They are all here to send us off," he explains.

"I'm so confused," Adele says, laughing nervously now.

"Don't be. You're going to love what he has in store for you," Anna says, hugging Adele and then Bart. Dario and Luca follow her and do the same.

"You two have fun. This will be so good for you," Sheila says and embraces them both.

"Bart," Andy says, hugging him. "Be safe and take care of this beautiful woman."

"I will. Thank you, Andy, for everything," he says.

Andy nods in acceptance of Bart's gratitude and, after hugging Adele, stands with the rest of the group again.

Frank and his wife are the last to give their farewells.

"I appreciate you, Frank. You're a gift," Bart says.

"It was a pleasure of mine," Frank says, then returns to the group.

Bart helps Adele into the carriage and then clambers in himself. He wraps an arm around her as the coachman shakes the reins, and the two horses pull them away. They both look back and wave at their friends, no, their *family,* Bart corrects himself.

When they are out of view, they sit back against the seat.

"Bart?" Adele asks.

"Yes?"

"Where are we going?"

"Home."

CHAPTER
Thirty

Adele

*H*ome. Padua. Adele's heart still races—even after a day of travel—at the thought of returning to their hometown. She imagines the streets she used to walk when she was only a child. The parks, the churches, and the shops. Most of all, she imagines the people, remembering their kindness and welcoming spirits. Padua is her home, or at least it was seventeen years ago. *Will anyone remember us?*

She quickly dismisses the intrusive thought and continues dreaming about what it will be like to enter the city for the first time since they left all those years ago.

Adele and Bart rock with the motion as the carriage makes its way through the countryside. The sun shines brightly through the small windows, spotlighting the floating dust particles in the air. Thankfully, Adele is wearing her most simple mantua—a pink dress without ruffles or frills so she can sit comfortably. Bart didn't plan well for the trip, she thinks. With his linen shirt and knee-length coat, he constantly has to reposition himself to be comfortable as he tries to sleep.

When Bart lets out a huff of defeat from his awkward and vain attempt at a nap, she looks at him with her soft gaze, face lit by a beam of sunlight. "Good morning, precious," she says sweetly but with a hint of sarcasm. "How was your nap?"

Bart clears his throat. "Please tell me I slept for hours, and we are in Padua now." He grimaces and rubs his lower back.

"I think you only dozed off for a couple of minutes. You should have worn something more comfortable," she says with a smirk.

He looks at her, disappointed.

"Sorry," she chuckles.

"It's not your fault I chose to wear nice but uncomfortable clothes."

"Here," Adele says, opening her arms. "Lay your head on my chest."

Bart hesitates for a second, then reclining against her, he pulls his feet up onto the seat. She runs her fingers through his brown hair, a few inches long, and massages his neck.

"Thank you," he says. "This feels good." His eyes are closed, and she watches as sleepiness begins filling him again.

Adele keeps her attention on her husband, reveling in his nearness, how he is curled against her like a child. His breathing falls into a steady rhythm, and she hopes he is able to fall asleep. The moment is peaceful. Memories of similar moments she shared with Cuori flood her mind, and for the first time, instead of the remembrance of her daughter swelling her throat with tears, she smiles.

"Bart?" she whispers.

"Yeah," he mumbles.

"Sometimes, I can still feel Cuori's finger tapping my arm to the beat of my heart."

Bart doesn't answer, and just when she thinks he might be asleep, he gently grasps her forearm, and with his index finger, he taps to the rhythm of her heartbeat. "Like this?" he asks.

Now her eyes flood with tears, but they are loving and grateful that Bart understands and possibly even shares the loveliness of this memory. *Just like that,* she thinks.

"I feel it all the time," he says and continues tapping until he drifts into sleep.

Although the carriage hasn't stopped yet, a knock on the hood from the coachman alerts Adele that they have arrived in Padua.

"Wake up, Bart. We are here," she says, giving him a shake.

He sits up, rubbing his eyes.

She stares out the window. "Look! We are on the Via Altinate. This is the street that takes us to the church in the middle of the city." She can scarcely contain herself. She wants to get out, feel the air, walk the familiar street. "Where is he dropping us off?" she asks Bart.

He looks at her gleefully. "You'll see."

Adele leans forward when the coach comes to a halt. She hears the coachman step down from his perch and a moment later, he opens the door to help Adele and Bart outside. Taking a few steps, Adele draws in her breath until her lungs reach full capacity and exhaling, she spins in a circle, her dress floating in the breeze she creates. "I missed the way you smell, Padua," she shouts, and smiles broadly.

Bart joins her with both their portmanteaus in hand. "It does smell better here." He thanks the coachman, pays him, and then leaves them standing in the middle of the street, captivated by their home city.

The sound of horses' hooves clopping signals the upcoming busy Sunday afternoon. "Let's step off the street," Bart says.

"Oh. Probably a good idea." She laughs, pulls her dress hem up off the ground, and walks quickly to the sidewalk. When she stops, a wave of nostalgia splashes her. "He dropped us off at the park!" she yells, drops her jaw, and then jogs onto the grass under the shade of the trees.

Bart leaves their trunks on the sidewalk and then runs to join her.

"This is where we grew up together. It is exactly the same, even after all the years that have passed," she says. "It's as if we are walking back in time."

"Such a special place," Bart says.

She turns her attention to him and notices his quiet excitement. His posture is tall and proud, and a persistent smile sits on his face. "Why did you bring us here first?" she asks, her curiosity growing.

He takes a focused and deep breath, then meets her gaze. "Ever since we lost Cuori, I've often questioned if life is worth living. I've felt stuck and consumed by my own pain." His face reddens, and tiny beads of sweat coat his forehead. "I haven't been a good husband. I haven't shown you how much I love you, how much I *still* love you."

"Stop it, Bart," she says. "We have already been through this."

He ignores her and continues. "Over the last two years, I have felt like time moves so slow I'll die, but then also moves so fast I can hardly breathe."

Feeling a rush of empathy, she understands perfectly every word he says. Her eyes burn with unshed tears.

"You are the reason I have survived until now. And you are the reason I'm always able to catch my breath. I am tired of surviving, though. I want us to heal together so we can *live* again," he finishes. Then he drops to one knee and takes both of her hands.

She presses her lips together to seal her mouth, and her heart begins to race. Sweat starts drenching the top of her head. Bart looks up at her with his golden-brown eyes, the same eyes that stole her heart a lifetime ago, and he asks, "Adele, my beautiful bride, will you marry me again?"

All she can hear now is the thud of her heart and blood pulsing through her ears. Her breath is stolen by shock, but still, she manages to say, "Yes!"

Bart stands and embraces her and, lifting her off her feet, he twirls her around. Her laugh mingles with his and echoes across the park. "Oh. I forgot," he says, reaching into his pocket. He pulls out a small case, opens it, and reveals a multicolored necklace made of multiple little beads. "This is for you," he says and ties it around her neck.

"It's lovely, Bart. Thank you," she says, then kisses him.

"You don't even know its meaning yet," he says with a magical tone.

"Really? What is it then?"

"The beads are made from the flowers that were atop Cuori's casket."

Adele loses her ability to speak. All she can do is study the necklace and think of Cuori. She leans on Bart and rests her head on his shoulder. Now she carries a bittersweet memory of her daughter around her neck.

She cries slow tears, which she had been holding back, soaking Bart's shoulder. It is a bit later when she dries her eyes and, looking over Bart's shoulder, notices a man and woman approaching them. She rubs her eyes and looks again. This time, she sees the face of a woman who holds a piece of her heart—a piece she has not seen in forever. The black hair, now sprinkled with gray, and the dark-olive skin and big-blue eyes of her best friend. *Molly!*

Adele quickly pushes Bart away and sprints toward Molly. Molly does the same, and when they meet, they kiss each other's cheeks and hold onto one another as if the world is trying to pull them apart again.

Her friend from childhood. The one who helped carry her through the loss of her mother—the woman who prayed with her for Cuori for twelve years. Adele realizes why Padua smells like home as they both hold each other. *Padua smells like Molly.*

CHAPTER
Thirty-one

Bart

Marco's and Molly's house stirs with anticipation. After they all eat breakfast—cooked by Marco—Adele and Molly take over the dining room table to discuss wedding plans, a nostalgic morning, to say the least.

"What about flowers? How many and what colors are you thinking?" Bart hears Molly asking Adele as he and Marco step outside, each with a mug of freshly steeped tea.

"So, how does it feel being back in Padua?" Marco asks, looking out into the city from the front porch.

Bart inhales deeply. "It is so much better even than I remember. I like Florence, but nowhere in the world could ever compare to home."

Talking to Marco isn't much different for Bart as it was seventeen years ago, as if he never moved away. Granted, they kept in touch through letters several times a year, just like Adele and Molly, but almost two decades without looking a friend in the eyes would make one worry the connection was lost.

"You shouldn't have waited so long to come back and visit. I had forgotten what you look like," Marco says, and they both laugh.

"You're the only man in Italy unafraid to grow your beard out as long as possible. I never forgot what you look like," Bart says and wraps an arm around Marco's shoulder. "You always looked scarier than you are."

"People who don't know me certainly think I am as scary as I look," Marco says, puffing up his chest.

"And when they get to know you?" Bart asks.

"Then they want a hug," Marco says, letting out a huff of air and returning to his normal posture.

"You can't blame them. Look at that gut. How they could resist hugging you," Bart teases.

Marco glares back at him with serious eyes. "I've earned this sexy body, don't make fun of it." He finishes with a full-bodied laugh, spilling some of his tea.

Bart grips his side as his chuckles cause him a side stitch.

"I can't help it. When you own a bakery, the dough ends up on your waistline no matter how hard you try not to eat it."

"Bakery?" he asks.

"Yeah. I need to show you something. Let's walk." They set their mostly empty mugs on the patio railing and head toward downtown Padua.

"Where are we going?" Bart asks along their stroll. Curious about the destination but even more inspired by their walk down memory lane. Every building and brick in the road give him a sense of comfort and familiarity.

"Remember when you left all those years ago, and I was unhappy with being at the leather shop?" Marco asks.

"Yes. Like it was yesterday."

"Well, a few years later, Sam took an interest in it. I always told myself I wouldn't force the business on him like my father did to me, but he genuinely enjoyed being there and leatherworking." Marco pauses a moment to catch his breath from talking and walking simultaneously. "Once he turned twenty and was married, I let him have it."

"I remember you said you gave the business to Sam. Is that when you started a bakery?" Bart asks.

"No, not exactly. I tried finding something to do with my life that interested me but found nothing. It turns out, though, I'm happy doing anything when I'm with Molly."

He gives Marco a confused look. "But Molly is your wife. You didn't already know you enjoyed being around her?"

"Nope. You know how I was so caught up in how much I hated my life?" Marco says.

"I remember."

"Because of that I was unaware of the diamond I had been married to the whole time. So, when I realized I was content with being with Molly, I asked her what she wanted to do. I knew she loved baking and wasn't surprised when she said she wanted to open a bakery," Marco finishes, and as if planned perfectly, they arrive directly in front of Molly's Homemade Bread & Pastries.

"What a beautiful storefront," Bart says.

Large windows in front show off the tables and chairs inside. Chalk on the outside of the windows details the weekly discounts, and overflowing flower baskets on the sidewalk make him think of Adele's love for flowers.

"Thank you," Marco says, pulling a key from his back pocket to open the front door. He gives Bart a full tour of the bakery, the flour and sugar stores in the back, and a custom-built wood-fired oven. The aroma of vanilla and rising bread is almost intoxicating.

"Smells divine in here," he says.

"I gain weight just from the aroma," Marco says, chuckling.

"So, the business does well?" Bart asks.

"It does. Pays all of our bills. And I am able to spend all day, every day, with the woman I love, so how could it not be a thriving business?"

Bart smiles at his beaming friend. "I am so happy for you, Marco. Why did you never mention this in your letters?"

"There are just some things meant to be experienced in person. A letter could not express the specialness of this place. But more than that, Molly and I didn't want you and Adele to worry about us or feel pressured to visit since we opened a business. We knew how busy with your own lives you were."

"It is amazing to be here and have a tour of it from you, but I wish you would have told us so we could have been celebrating with you."

Marco doesn't say anything for a moment. Then he pulls out a couple of blueberry muffins and hands one to Bart. "I don't mean to make the conversation too serious or awkward, but how have you been, Bart? When you told us you were coming a few months ago we were so excited and then you show up here seemingly happy and ready to renew your vows to Adele—which is beautiful—but as your friend, I need to ask what is really going on with you." Marco gestures for Bart to take a seat. "Although I want to believe everything is going well, I'm just not that naïve."

Bart sits and takes a bite out of the muffin. When he is done chewing, he says, "I finished the piano."

Marco has already finished his muffin and, with wide eyes, asks, "Really?"

Bart nods. "The last two years, I have been entirely dedicated to building the piano. I figured out how it needed to be done, so it became easy. Going home to Adele was hard, not because I didn't love her, but because I knew we were growing apart little by little. We were both broken, and I didn't know what to say or do. But dedicating myself to something I understood and was now capable of doing was the obvious path for me to take."

Marco listens intently. "But now you're done."

"And now I'm done."

Marco nods.

"I didn't want to lose Adele, and she deserves better. I know she loves me the same as I love her. I didn't want to act like everything was okay between us. I knew we needed to rebuild our relationship, so where better to renew our vows than in the place we first committed to each other?"

Marco smiles and looks down at the table, then at Bart. "I think it is incredible."

He gazes out the bakery window onto the empty Sunday morning street. "Seeing her excitement when I brought her here and proposed again was all the confirmation I needed to know this was the right decision."

"How long are you planning to stay?"

"At least a couple of months. If that is alright with you? We have to be back in Florence by the new year for the event we'll hold to announce the debut of the piano. We're calling it The Creation of Music."

"Well, as for your visit, Molly and I are more than alright with being your hosts for the rest of this year," Marco says excitedly. "But tell me more about The Creation of Music?"

"It's the celebration the Florentine Court is planning to launch the piano. People from all across Italy will be there!" Bart says, feeling a rush of pride. "I would like for you and Molly to be there, too," he adds. "If you can."

Marco bobs his head. "Wouldn't miss it. We will just close the bakery while we are gone."

Bart smiles, feeling the warmth even on the inside. His friend is hardly the same as he remembers, but happier, successful, and even easier to talk to. *I wonder if he thinks I have changed.*

Marco and Bart visit together in the bakery, sharing a couple more blueberry muffins before Marco locks up and they head back. Marco doesn't ask Bart anything about Cuori, which is a relief for him.

As they walk home, Marco steps onto a side street with small apartment-style houses on both sides. "Why are we going this way?" he asks.

"I think there is something you would like to see."

The street brings waves of familiar but unspecific emotions to his mind. A few minutes later, and it's like a hammer to his heart; both painful and beautiful memories overwhelm him. His chest hurts at the sight, but his eyes long to continue taking in the view.

His childhood home stands proudly, precisely as it did forty years ago. Somehow, he had forgotten it existed. It had no place in his life anymore. When he and Adele were married, he tried to forget about it, although living in Padua he was constantly reminded of it.

His strongest recollection is of his mother and baby brother both dying, and no part of him wants to remember it. He doesn't want to face the fact that he never processed the loss of his mother or the anger he has for his father emotionally abandoning him. How could he have processed it? He was only a child.

"Want to go inside?" Marco asks.

Bart turns his head sharply. "How? Who lives here now?"

"Sam."

"Really?" he says in disbelief.

"Yeah. Let's go." Marco sets off and Bart follows in his wake, heart beating fast. When his palms become clammy, he wipes them on his pants, but it doesn't help. *I don't know if I can do this.*

The exterior is freshly painted in the original clay-red color, and the steps and railing are the same.

Marco knocks on the front door, and when Sam opens it, he is wearing a bright smile, leaving Bart no choice but to go inside and face his past head-on.

CHAPTER
Thirty-two

Adele

"*I* don't know, Molly. What if nobody comes?" Adele complains as Molly suggests various food options for the wedding reception.

"Are you crazy? The whole town will be there. Everyone is excited for you," Molly chirps.

"We just arrived yesterday. How do they know we are here?"

"Adele, I started telling everyone you were coming back to renew your vows as soon as we received Bart's letter a couple of months ago."

"So, people *actually* care about an old couple renewing their vows?" She isn't surprised Molly has told everyone though.

"Probably more so than a newlywed. There is so much more to celebrate with renewing vows anyway. There is both history *and* future to be grateful for," Molly says, her high energy spilling onto Adele.

"That is true," she contemplates. "Okay! Let's do a whole pastry table," she says, laughing.

"There we go! Now that is what I'm talking about," Molly says, then stands from the table. "Let's take a break."

Adele stands up and nods in agreement. She follows Molly through her house, admiring her decorations and dramatic style. Her gown itself is vibrant, with every color of the rainbow sewn together; she undoubtedly took inspiration from the story of Joseph when making it.

They step outside onto the back patio, and the first thing to catch Adele's eyes is Molly's garden. Its measly nature compares in no way to Adele's, but still, it's healthy and full of fragrant herbs. She takes a long inhale, the Padua air still intoxicating. "I've missed your backyard. Look how the trees have grown!" Adele gasps and points, not remembering them like this at all.

Molly turns to her with a disapproving face. "Adele," she says, shaking her head. "This is not the house we lived in before. These trees are over 100 years old, and our first house didn't even have sprouts," she explains, her tone dripping with sarcasm.

Oh. "I was wondering why nothing felt familiar," she says, scoffing at herself.

"Adele. You were not. You thought this was the same house we lived in twenty years ago," Molly says, not being fooled.

"Fine. But I have never said I was an observant person." Adele laughs.

"I hope not. Because you didn't even realize this is the house you and Bart lived in."

Adele's eyes widen with surprise. "There is no way. I would have known that." *Maybe it is, though.*

"It is. We just painted it a different color a few years ago," Molly says.

"You know, it's kind of coming back to me now," she says, looking all around to see the more minor details. "I can't believe I didn't recognize it sooner."

Molly punches her arm, and Adele glares back at her with her jaw open while recovering her footing. "Ouch. Why did you hit me?"

Molly leans her head forward to speak. "This is not your old house," she says with her contagious cackle. "You haven't changed a bit, Adele, as gullible as always."

Adele hasn't spent time with Molly in so long. Her first response is to act defensively, but she remembers it would only encourage her more. She waits for Molly to finish laughing, then says, "You better watch it. I remember some embarrassing moments involving you, too."

Molly squints, trying to see her bluff. "You don't have anything on me."

Adele pulls her shoulders back and steps closer to Molly. "Are you sure you want to test me?"

Molly smiles. "Nope."

"That's what I thought," Adele says, and her sense of satisfaction is tempered with relief. She had nothing on her friend.

Molly sobered. "I do want to know something, though. And I want you to be honest."

"I will be," she responds. Sensing Molly's heart, she braces herself for the hard conversation surfacing. Her letters to Molly since Cuori's death have been brief, so she has much to tell her friend.

"How have you been? I know we've been reminiscing and laughing, but you lost your Cuori, and I want to know you're still alive on the inside."

She isn't surprised by Molly's question or the sudden tears dripping off her chin. "Not very good. It's been like waking up in hell every day, pulling myself out just to do it all over again the next day."

Molly's face softens, and she grasps both of Adele's hands. "I've been worried about you."

She nods and relaxes in her friend's embrace. Molly is a friend but also a firm foundation, a source of beloved memories.

Molly was with Adele through every miscarriage and prayed with her every day. If it weren't for Molly, she might have lost hope and never given birth to Cuori. She lets slow tears continue to fall as she leans on Molly.

"Tell me about her. Describe how beautiful she was, how smart and talented. I want to hear *everything* about her. Your letters did a good job, but I know there must be so much more."

"Okay."

"Come." Molly squeezes Adele's hand. "Let's sit on the bench there." She gestures toward an old and towering shade tree. "Marco built it, and it is my favorite place to sit."

Adele lets Molly lead her, both dreading and pleased for the opportunity to talk about her beautiful daughter. "You would have loved her," Adele tells Molly as they sit facing one another. "She was feisty and had a sarcastic sense of humor. It's obvious God heard your prayers louder than mine," she says, chuckling.

Molly throws her head back in laughter. "This makes me so happy."

Adele rolls her eyes. "Her hair and skin was a perfect mix of mine and Bart's. Her locks shone with a hint of gold in the sunlight but was rich in deep auburn color. Her skin was a light olive, always glowing. And her eyes, oh her eyes." Adele presses her fingertips to her mouth. "Her hazel-green eyes were the most gorgeous eyes in the world." Her voice rises and becomes unsteady.

"It sounds like she was more beautiful than an angel," Molly says softly.

She nods and sniffs to clear her nose. "She was, and just as beautiful was her art. She could draw or paint anything, and it would be better than seeing it in real life."

"Really?" Molly asks.

"Yes. She was incredible. Her room is full of painted canvases. She gave many of them away as gifts. There is even a shop in Florence that has one on display," Adele says. Feeling proud of her daughter.

"Was painting her favorite thing to do?"

"Yes. And reading. She would be reading anytime she wasn't painting."

"Sounds like she was brilliant."

"In every way. She was much smarter than me. She got Bart's intelligence for sure."

"A person with your looks and Bart's brains would be hard to describe. I so wish I could have met her."

She looks at Molly. "I'm sorry we never came back. I don't know why—"

"Hush. I'm sorry too. We never came to see or visit you either, so both of us are guilty. Life demands so much from us that we have no time—or money—to think of visiting other cities. Some years were spent just trying to survive. I'm so glad you're here now, though. I've missed you more than you know the last seventeen years," Molly says with a comforting smile at the end.

"You have no idea, Molly. You were my best friend and still are. I will never forget how lonely I was when we first left."

"I remember, too. Your letters broke my heart."

Adele doesn't speak for a moment, then says, "You and Marco seem happy?"

"Happy isn't the word for it," Molly says excitedly. "We are in love like we've never been before."

"Really?" Adele straightens eager to hear more.

"When Sammy took over the leather shop, we opened the bakery together and rediscovered our love. We had forgotten the reasons we liked each other, but when we started spending so much time together, we remembered exactly why we fell in love and have even more reasons now."

"I am so happy!" Adele puts a hand over her heart. "I am so very happy for you."

"Thank you. It was a long journey, but worth every step." She pauses a moment to look away, then looking back, she says, "Am I right to think that you and Bart haven't been doing so well?"

Adele sighs. "It's been a long and terrible two years. I could probably count on one hand the number of meaningful conversations the two of us have had in that span of time. The majority of them having occurred in the last few days," she adds.

"That breaks my heart, Adele. You can work it out, though, right?"

Adele shifts her glance, observing Molly's garden. "Yes. I believe we can. I believe we will. We both want it. We still love each other. It's just that grief tore us apart, but perhaps love can put us back together. With a few scars, of course, but whole again."

"How beautiful. I have no doubt love will reconnect you. The wedding will be a wonderful celebration."

"You really think so?" Adele is not so certain.

"How could you doubt it?" Molly asks. "Like I already said, renewing vows is worth celebrating even more than the original marriage!" She stands up. "Let's go start dinner."

Adele lets Molly draw her to her feet. "But I feel bad. I don't like too much attention or people to burden themselves for me." She follows Molly down the path to the house.

"Yeah, right. We're women, and we love attention. It's what God made us for. Eyes have to look somewhere. Why not us?"

Adele laughs, thinking Molly *is not wrong.* "I could definitely use the validation."

"Exactly."

"What will we make for supper?" Adele asks.

"Same as always."

"Still pizza?"

Molly looks at her, acting confused. "As if there could be anything else."

She laughs. "Pizza it is, then!" *I have missed days like this.*

CHAPTER
Thirty-three

Bart
Five Weeks Later – December

Almost every candle in Padua stretches out over the grassy area. Bart decorates a small park along the Bacchiglione River, not much larger than a gentle stream. A moss-covered arched bridge provides a walkway to the green grass shaded by the spreading canopy of an ancient umbrella tree. Marco helps him tie countless candles to the tree's lowest branches and places many on the bridge railings as well. December weather in Padua is unpredictable, but luckily today it's the warmest and least windy it's been in a couple weeks.

"She is going to love this." Marco finishes tying a knot around one of the tree limbs.

"I can't wait." Bart focuses on balancing candles.

"You're making my life more difficult, though."

"How so?"

"You come here and do all this romantic stuff for Adele, probably raising Molly's expectations for me. Now I have to figure out how to meet or exceed an outdoor, candlelit picnic under the stars along the river." Marco sighs dramatically.

Bart grins. "It was getting too easy for you. Someone had to raise the bar a little bit."

"No. The bar was perfect. My height."

"I'm borrowing a guitar from my old shop, too. I'm going to play a song for her," Bart says, smirking.

"How fantastic. Now you're just showing off."

"You know I've always been a sucker for romantic moments. How could you expect anything less from me?" he asks, stepping out from under the tree to examine their work.

"I'm not surprised. This entire setting screams your name." Marco laughs.

"I hope Adele is surprised, though," he says. The time they have had together here in Padua has been indescribable. The beginning of a healing journey both of them are fully committed to traveling.

"She won't be," Marco says, and when Bart glances at him, Marco cocks his head and says, "but she will act like she is," and they both laugh.

"I have never done anything quite this big before, so she will definitely still be surprised. Besides, she is distracted by our wedding tomorrow. She'll never see this coming."

"You're right," Marco admits. "She will be awestruck. Especially once nightfall arrives, and Molly and I light all the candles for you. This place will be mesmerizing."

The two of them admire their hard work. The candles they placed on the ground create a pathway to the quilt, which lies open on the grass just out from under the canopy of the tree.

"The sun is sinking pretty low. You ready to head back?" Marco asks.

"Yeah, it'll be dusk soon."

Arriving at Marco's house, they find Molly in the kitchen alone. She clasps both hands together in excitement when she sees them. "What took so long?" she whispers.

Marco points to Bart. "He had to use every candle in this city."

Molly smiles at Bart. "She has no idea what is going on. I'm so happy for you," she says as she walks past them both and stands at the door. She turns her attention to Marco. "What are you standing there for? Let's go."

Marco obeys her orders and puts his hand on Bart's shoulder before leaving. "Good luck, friend. See you in a few."

He gives Marco a grateful expression in response. "Thank you!" he says, waving bye to Molly.

Marco follows her out of the house, and before the door shuts all the way, Molly pokes her head inside and whispers, "The picnic basket is on the counter, full of food and ready to go!"

"Thank you!" he whispers, and the front door finally closes, leaving Bart alone.

He is still for a few moments, planning the night ahead of him one last time. *It should be simple: Guitar will be dropped off soon, and Molly and Marco will have all the candles lit. And Adele still has no clue.*

His thoughts are immediately cut off when Adele walks around the corner in a lavender-purple dress. *How does she always glow even when she isn't standing in the sunlight?*

"Hey," she says a bit awkwardly. "What are you doing?"

He smiles. "Admiring you." He approaches her with graceful steps and wraps his arms around her waist.

"You're sweet. But really? Also, where did Molly go?" she asks.

"I just got back from town with Marco, and as soon as we came in, Molly asked Marco if he was ready, and they left," he says, trying to be believable.

"That is odd. Molly has been acting strange all day. I wonder where she needed to go?"

"I know, right? Marco too. Very weird. Very, very weird," he says. *Too much.*

Adele looks at him with doubtful eyes but then brushes it off. "We didn't prepare anything for supper. Is there anything in particular you want?" she asks, picking up a pile of bed linens from the chair.

"No need to make anything. We're going on a picnic," he says, his heart beginning to race. *Relax. Don't blow it.*

Adele glances at him with a confused face. "A picnic? At night?"

"Yeah. It'll be fun. Just a little thing."

She pauses with a contemplative expression for a minute, trying to work out the situation in her mind. "Something is going on, but I can't put my finger on it."

Bart paces around the room to calm his fidgeting hands. "Adele," he tilts his head and beams at her, "there is nothing to figure out. It's just a picnic under the stars with your husband."

"Fine. Whatever. Should I change?"

"No. You look perfect."

"Okay, let's go," she says, walking toward him.

"No. We have to wait until it's dark," he says, stopping her.

"Seriously? Why?"

"Too many questions, Adele," he says with a modest laugh. Trying to sound casual.

She glares at him. Seemingly annoyed.

"Sorry. But we do need to wait for a little bit," he explains.

Adele crosses her arms. "Fine. How was your day?"

"It was good," he says. The room is quiet and tense, his nervous excitement making him sweat. "Yours?"

"Good," she says.

Silence hangs in the air, both standing in Marco and Molly's kitchen, waiting for the sun to set. He can feel the disinterest emanating from Adele. Why is she not in a good mood today? he wonders.

"Okay. Let's go." His simmering surprise and Adele's impatience is causing too much tension for him to bear.

"But you said we had to wait?" Adele questions him.

"We can take the long way there," he says, picking up the basket of food Molly prepared and then opening the front door, gesturing for Adele to go out first, and he follows her.

"Which way?" she asks. Arms still crossed.

"Let's go to the right," he says, and they begin walking in the opposite direction of the park. Bart wants to give Marco and Molly more than enough time to light all the candles.

His nervousness leaves him as they stroll along the ancient brick streets of Padua, but Adele still exudes slight anger. "My love, are you alright?" he finally asks.

Adele turns to him with annoyed eyes but then lets her shoulders relax when she begins talking. "The wedding is in the morning, and I am so anxious about it."

"How come? Aren't you excited?"

"It means so much to both of us, and I want it to go well, but I feel like it will be a scattered mess, and nobody will show up, which will be embarrassing," she says with no breath between.

"There is no reason to worry. The church will have everything set up for us, and even if just Molly and Marco come, they would be enough."

"I know," she sighs. "I'm overthinking it. But Molly was in a weird mood all day today. Now you're refusing to explain yourself or where we are going, and I do not have the patience for this tonight," she says, speaking with her hands.

Bart leans over and kisses her on the cheek. "It will all make sense soon."

She turns her head toward him again, this time with softer eyes. "You know I don't enjoy secrets, Bart."

"This isn't a secret, but another surprise. One which you are about to experience, but not at this moment," he explains with a crooked grin.

Adele can't help but smile back at him. She exhales. "Okay. I trust you."

"Thank you."

"It better be good, though," she adds.

"Or what?" he asks, sensing her lightheartedness.

"It's a surprise," she says, purposely not looking at him as they walk, leaving him to wonder. But he can see her smirk from the side of her face.

I kind of want to know what it is now, he thinks. Feeling more comfortable with every step they take together.

The park where the picnic is set up is only a ten-minute walk from Marco and Molly's house, but Adele and Bart take nearly an hour, arriving at the street that leads to the bridge when it is almost entirely dark.

Before they round the last corner, passing the final building, Bart stops Adele and turning her to face him, he says, "This is it."

Adele doesn't say anything, only smiles. He holds the picnic basket in his left hand and Adele's hand in his right, and they walk around the corner where the bridge and the tree lit by hundreds of candles come into view. He can hear Adele's breathing become quicker as they draw closer to the scene.

When they approach the bridge, she covers her mouth with her hand. He glances at her, then at Marco and Molly, standing in front of the bridge. "Thank you," he whispers to them as they hug. Molly hugs Adele, who is still speechless and crying now.

"Enjoy your evening, you two," Molly whispers and then waves as she and Marco leave.

Adele pulls her hand from Bart so she can lean over the bridge. The river below reflects the flickering candles in its current. The reflection is so detailed that even the melted wax dripping down the candle's body is shown.

After they cross the bridge and follow the path of candles to the quilt on the grass, Bart sets the basket of food down and watches Adele as she gazes at the tree, seemingly on fire. Her eyes absorb the flames, slightly reflective like the river but far more brilliant.

"Bart," she says softly. "This looks like heaven." She spins herself around. Her dress catches the breeze, and floats around her angelically. She stops briefly and closes her eyes, and he can barely hear her as she whispers into the night, "This place is almost perfect, baby girl. The only thing it's missing is you."

Now he cries, having kept himself collected until now. Adele meets him where he stands, and they embrace each other amid the warm, ambient light. There is something else here too, under the tree, hidden in the air. *Love*, he thinks.

Adele notices the guitar on its stand next to the quilt and picnic basket when they let go of each other. She gasps. "You're going to play too?"

"No. I'm going to play *and* sing to you," he says with pride. All his preparation for this evening over the last few weeks gives him confidence.

Adele covers her mouth again, new tears collecting in her eyes. "You are overwhelming me. I don't know what to say."

He leans toward her. "You don't have to say anything, only soak it up." He stretches out his hand, she takes it, and he helps her sit on the ground comfortably. Then, he reaches for the guitar, and on one knee, he begins gently picking the strings, forming heart-wrenchingly beautiful notes and chords.

"Our time we have had back in Padua inspired this song a few days after we got here, but I've been waiting for the right time to give it to you," he says. Then, with a smile, he adds, "I think tonight is the right time." He turns his attention back to his hands and the instrument.

After he plays a few rounds of the chord progression, he hums to clear his throat and begins pouring his heart out to his wife in the form of a melody.

We were young
But we knew that it was good.
You stole my heart, I wanted you to.
Since then, all I've wanted was to be with you.
I have learned
The sound of love is your heart beating.
Now I know
You're the reason life is worth living.
Though time has been unkind
It is our love that holds us together.
We've been through hell

Too many times for us to count.
Yet here we are, still in love.
Nothing could ever keep us apart.
I have found
Beauty defined within your eyes.
Now I see
I'm the richest man in the world.
Though time has been unkind
It is our love that holds us together.
I love you.
I love you.
I love you.

His voice is soft and rich in natural vibrato. When he finishes the song, he is out of breath, his racing heart stealing all his oxygen. Adele waits for him to set the guitar aside, and then she lunges toward him, wrapping both arms around him as he falls backward to the ground and kisses him. "I love you too," she says, then shifting herself off of him, she lies on her back beside him.

A warm and intimate silence grows between them as they gaze at the night sky.

"Thank you," Adele murmurs. "That was the most special gift in the world."

He gazes into her alluring eyes, still fascinated with her beauty even after thirty years. "You are welcome. It doesn't do justice to how I feel about you, but then again, nothing really can."

Adele beams and turns her attention back to the sky, filled with blazing color and blocked by only a few dark spots from the floating clouds. Together, they watch the stars shine and the candles around them burn. The gentle sounds of the river to their left could easily lull them to sleep.

The crickets chirp near the water's edge, and the last few fireflies of the autumn season dance over the grass, their glow reflecting on the water's surface just like the candle flames. This is no ordinary night in Padua, but magic fills the air. *True love is never lost, only refined,* Bart thinks. It takes many shapes throughout the course of its life, but every form is beautiful.

[Listen to 'Our Love']

CHAPTER
Thirty-four

Adele

*T*he church is exactly the same as it was almost thirty years ago when she first married Bart. Now, she is here to do it again. Excitement fills her bones, but not the same kind of excitement as the first wedding. This time, she is *more* nervous. She worries people will judge her graying hair and freckled skin from all the years she has spent in the sun working in the garden, not to mention she has gained some weight from when she was a teenager.

Despite the worry within her, last night with Bart made her realize she is more in love this time. Maybe love is similar to a muscle. When it is broken down and then healed, it becomes even stronger than before. *I know Bart thinks I am pretty. Who cares what other people think?* she tells herself over and over again.

Molly comes back into the dressing room to fluff her flowing dress and wish her good luck before she goes to find her seat. "There are so many people here," she says, beaming.

"You're lying?" Adele asks.

Molly shakes her head. "My friend, you are more beautiful now than you were thirty years ago."

Adele looks at her stomach. "Yeah, right. I have more rolls on my belly now, and not the cute and tasty kind you can eat."

"Hey, we've both earned our extra layers of insulation. Own it." Molly says, and they both lose their composure in laughter. After wiping away a tear of joy, she says, "I'm leaving, but Marco will be here in a moment to walk you down the aisle."

Once Molly exits the room, leaving Adele alone, she takes a deep breath, and a few seconds later a knock announces Marco's presence. "Are you ready, Adele?" he calls softly.

"Yes." She opens the door, greeting him. "Marco, you look so handsome." He really does, she thinks, dressed as he is in a dark doublet.

He blushes, thanking her. "But, Adele, you are stunning, more brilliant than a star in your white dress."

Now she is the one to blush. "Thank you, Marco."

When he offers his arm, she takes it, and they begin their trek to the entrance of the sanctuary.

The chandelier in the foyer distributes glimmers in the rays of sunlight. The room is dyed every color of the rainbow from the enormous stained-glass window. The marble floors echo their footsteps, matching her pounding heart's rhythm.

They surmount the small stairway to two colossal wooden doors. They are opened wide, and she can see the pews are crowded with people on both sides of the aisle. Spotting her, they begin to stand, signaling others to do the same.

The harp and organ begin to play, and she and Marco start taking slow but steady steps toward the stage. When they enter the sanctuary, Adele feels the crowd's heat enfold her, threatening to make her sweat. The sight of Bart after a few steps calms her racing heart. *You are my rock.* She studies him, his hard-earned wrinkles and gray hair make him all the more handsome. His round and kind face is still her favorite place to rest her eyes.

She recognizes many faces among the attendees, and every one of them is looking at her with warmth and love, filling her with a little more joy with each step she takes. Her nervousness is gone now, her fear of judgment eradicated, replaced by excitement and gratitude for how much she has been blessed. *All these people are here to celebrate with us. I can't believe it!*

Arriving at another staircase, this one leading up to the stage, Adele imagines the elegant sweep of the train of her dress as she climbs up to where Bart awaits her. When she at last stands before him, she can see the tears falling down his face. She is unsurprised by her own suddenly burning her eyes, and she happily lets her tears fall. Over the last two years, she has learned that tears feel so good when they aren't being held back.

Marco gives Adele away to Bart, leaving the two standing together on the stage. Adele locks Bart's gaze, staring into the eyes of the man she loves.

He takes her hands. "You're more beautiful than an angel."

"That is exactly what you said when we did this the first time," she whispers.

"And it is still true, even more so now."

As the final chords of the tune the harpist is playing fade, the priest arrives on the stage. "The bride and groom have prepared their own vows," he announces and gestures that the crowd should sit.

A hush falls over the sanctuary and Adele can feel that every ear is tuned to hear the exchange of vows she and Bart have written.

"Adele," the priest says softly.

She takes a deep breath in an attempt to keep her heartbeat from exploding. Her face is warm, and she senses it is bathed in the kaleidoscope of colors that stream through the stained-glass windows that line the wall behind her. "Bart," she begins. "I remember the moment we first met as children. I thought you were the most handsome boy in the whole world. You told me you wanted to be an inventor, and I could see the passion in your eyes then, and I see it the same now. Not only are you passionate about inventing, though, but also about being a good husband and a father." Her voice catches, and she looks down, tightening her teeth against her ready tears.

A moment later, more composed, she lifts her eyes to Bart and continues. "Your love is both gentle and strong, and you have taken care of me far better than I deserve. You were the most perfect father to Cuori. Her heart and mind grew in endlessly beautiful ways because as her papa, you encouraged her to dream. I am so privileged to have shared being a parent with you, and together, we raised the most beautiful daughter." Her throat narrows with emotion, but she pushes the remainder of her wedding vow through. "She is in heaven with Jesus now. We are still here, but it won't be long when we see her again. Until then, Bart, I can't wait to spend the rest of my life falling more in love with you." As she finishes, she hears a murmur whisper through the crowd and looking out, she sees that many are having to wipe away tears. She manages a smile before bringing her gaze back to Bart, and while he appears emotionally distraught, he is beaming.

The priest gives the couple and the audience a few moments to collect themselves and then addressing Bart, he says quietly, "You may begin when you are ready."

Bart straightens and, squeezing her hands, he begins. "Adele. My love. My bride. My heart. No name can do justice for who you are."

As he speaks, Adele sees him as she did last night, his face suffused in a candlelight glow as he serenaded her in a voice that melted into her ears like butter on a biscuit. Smooth and rich.

"I have dreamed since I was a child of being an inventor, of building something significant. For a long time, I thought it was the harpsichord, then the pianoforte, and then the piano, an instrument that would change music forever, but really, it was you and me. The life we have built together. Hell threw its best at us, yet we survived. Life took our daughter away from us, yet we remain unbroken, healed, and stronger than before."

Bart's voice rings with authenticity and confidence, and Adele's heart soars with love and pride.

"We both know life is unfair, and perhaps it's still not done with us, but I know with certainty we will endure, bearing the pain of whatever is to come together. We will merely be refined by such travails, like a diamond. Adele, you are the reason I didn't give up on the piano. You are the reason I didn't give up on myself when we lost Cuori."

Now, when his voice catches, she squeezes his hands in reassurance.

His jaw clenches, and he continues speaking. "I can't wait to spend the rest of my life continuing to build the only thing that really matters: a life with you."

She hasn't cried, but now that he is finished talking, tears spill down her cheeks, a hot flood, and a moment later they are in one another's arms.

"You may kiss the bride!" the priest shouts.

Without hesitating, Bart obeys, and at first his kiss is gentle, but it soon swells with growing passion. The crowd comes to its feet and Adele hears the applause breaking around her like thunder; voices follow raised in a cacophony of praise for the couple and their renewed avowal to each other and to the lifetime of their love.

Marco and Molly are first to join Adele and Bart on the altar. "That was beautiful, you two," Molly says, sniffling as she hugs them. Then she turns to the crowd and shouts, "Everyone is invited to the reception, which begins now at the park across the street."

The four of them wait until the sanctuary has emptied before they walk to the reception, where at least a hundred people are waiting to congratulate them and indulge in pastries from Molly's Bakery.

Nostalgia once again fills the park. Adele feels it in every fiber of her being. The only change from thirty years ago that she can see is the signs of aging amidst the crowd, but there is also a love that has proven itself greater than anything life could throw at it.

CHAPTER
Thirty-five

1700 – Bart
Friday, January 1st

Molly and Marco sit opposite Bart and Adele in the carriage bound for Florence. Adele has fallen asleep on Bart's shoulder, but Bart, Molly and Marco are wakeful, only occasionally breaking the clop of the horse's hooves with a bit of conversation. Bart is glad for his friends' company. After spending a full two months together in Padua, Molly and Marco said they could not face an emotional farewell and decided to travel with the Cristoforis where they would attend The Creation of Music celebration. Word of the event has been printed in newspapers in every major city throughout Italy, including Padua. Only the famous and wealthy are guaranteed seats in the music hall for the piano's unveiling, but every citizen is invited to witness it, though they might have to stand and have a limited viewing angle.

The unveiling is taking place tomorrow, Saturday, January 2, 1700, at noon. Andy had written to Bart that he felt that starting the new year with music leading the way would bring people hope and unity amidst a chaotic world where peace and common interests are hard to come by. Looking out now at the passing landscape, Bart thinks how he has missed Andy. *It will be good to see him again.*

A bit later, when the coachman knocks on the carriage and shouts, "Almost to the city!" Adele jerks upright.

"We're here," he tells her softly, patting her arm to reassure her. He watches her rub her eyes and fix her hair. "Have a good nap?" he asks.

She yawns. "Yeah, pretty good."

"I don't know how," Molly says. "I would have a horrible crick in my neck if I slept like that."

Adele lifts her arms in an exaggerated stretch and, looking through the carriage window, she says, "Oh, look. You can see the whole city from up here!"

Bart follows her glance as the carriage begins its descent from atop the last hill before entering the city below.

Molly says, "Wow. Marco, you have to see this."

He leans over her for a better view. "Florence is huge," he says in surprise. He turns a wide-eyed gaze to Bart. "Weren't you two scared the first time you saw it?"

"Terrified," Bart answers. "But it doesn't feel as big once you're inside it."

Adele and Bart exchange a knowing smile, sharing a mutual pleasure in watching their friends be captivated by the view of Florence, a place they've learned to call home, the same as Padua.

When they arrive at the Cristofori household, they unload their trunks, pay the coachman, and step inside just as the sun is beginning to set. Sheila has stayed at their home for the last two months, keeping it clean and the garden tended to. She must be out running errands, Bart assumes, because she isn't there when they step inside. *It's as if we never left,* Bart thinks as Adele gives Molly a quick tour.

"This is a beautiful home, Bart," Marco compliments.

"Thank you. Want to sit outside?"

"Sure."

Bart and Marco step back outside onto the porch and sit facing the pink and purple sunset pouring over the city's red roofs.

"Are you nervous about tomorrow?" Marco asks.

"I am now. I haven't been until today, but now I'm worried something will go wrong," he admits.

"Like what?"

Bart shrugs his shoulders. "I don't even know. If there was a problem, Andy would have postponed the event. So, there is no reason for me to be nervous."

"There is always a reason to be anxious, though the reason often exists only in your mind. You just have to choose whether or not it is worth your peace," Marco says.

Bart nods. "Yeah."

"I am so proud to have you as a friend, and I am excited to witness all that tomorrow holds. It will go smoothly, and everything will be fine."

Bart's anxious mind calms as he realizes all the support he has. "Thank you, Marco. I needed that. I guess since so many people will be there tomorrow, I was concerned about their opinions and whether or not they would be impressed. But honestly, I only really want the opinions of those I care about."

"You're welcome. Besides, you won't see most of the people there ever again anyway, so who cares what they think," Marco laughs.

"Yeah. Who cares," Bart laughs, too.

CHAPTER
Thirty-six

1700 – Bart
Saturday, January 2ⁿᵈ

"Actually, I care a lot," Bart whispers aloud as they approach the music hall. He and Adele lead a small crowd: Marco and Molly, Anna, Dario, Luca, and Sheila. They watch as an enormous crowd waits for the doors to open. "The event doesn't start for another two hours. This is crazy," he says, voice shaking.

Adele grasps his hand. "It's okay. You were already expecting a lot of people. They've just arrived early is all."

Bart nods. "Follow me. We will go in through the back of the building." He leads his small group across the street and around the music hall to find a crowd-free entrance. Holding the door open, he lets all of them pass him, and instructs them to walk the length of the hallway. Now, he is at the back of the group, and when they pass by his shop, he stops for a moment to look inside. The piano is gone, the room empty, and as he stares into it, his mind fills with a mix of his memories, both wonderful and dark. Here is a place where he invented an instrument, destroyed it, and then rebuilt it as the piano, fully realized. He does not know how long has passed, but on hearing Adele shout his name he runs to catch up to everyone.

Inside the auditorium, he is overwhelmed at the seemingly endless rows of chairs that fill the space. He notices Andy and Frank standing in front of the stage, and on catching sight of him, Frank waves at him.

Bart beckons at his group. "Over here," he tells them.

"Bart, you stranger," Andy says, drawing him into a hug. "I was beginning to worry you were going to miss it."

"I couldn't possibly," Bart says as Frank gives his hand a hearty shake. "We definitely should have arrived sooner, though."

"Crowd is huge, huh?" Andy chuckles at Bart's expression, correctly reading his apprehension. "Aren't you excited for the world to witness your masterpiece?"

"Yes and no," he answers.

"No need to stress. Today is all about you and what you have done, but you don't have to do or say anything. The piano will speak for you now."

Bart nods, catching the wave of Andy's enthusiasm.

Once Andy has greeted Adele with a hug, Bart introduces Marco and Molly to him and Frank. He's barely finished, when Andy, looking across the room at someone waving their hand, says, "Looks like they are letting people in. Our seats are over here." He guides them up the steps and onto the stage to a row of chairs where Frank's wife is already sitting.

"Wait," Bart says, frightened. "We are sitting on the stage?"

"Well, yeah," Frank says elbowing Bart's side. "You deserve to have the best view of both the piano and the crowd. Don't you agree?"

"You're not sitting alone," Adele whispers into his ear.

Looking around, Bart finds he has a perfect view of the piano, where it sits beaming at the center of the stage. The last oil coating he applied to the wood before leaving for Padua has soaked in and aged slightly, so it no longer reflects the light but absorbs it, causing it to glow.

They all find their seats on the far left of the stage and watch as the crowd begins shuffling in. Bart watches, mesmerized, as the lower levels and mezzanine fills up quickly, then the balconies too. Once every seat is occupied, people stand shoulder to shoulder against the auditorium's back wall and cram into the music hall lobby, willing to stand to have a partial view of the performance.

Responding to a signal Bart doesn't catch, Andy rises from his chair, and Bart thinks how grand he looks, wearing his prestigious white wig, and walking with utmost confidence. When Andy arrives at the piano the room falls silent except for the subtle sound of breath rising and falling from the audience. Bart's heart is beating so loudly, he is amazed no one can hear it. His mouth dries as he watches Andy carefully open and raise the piano's lid. The auditorium is built to naturally project sound from the stage, and lifting the piano's lid, Bart knows, will only further amplify the rich melodies.

Now, turning to face them all, Andy says in a strong, clear voice, "On behalf of the Florentine Court, myself, Andrea de' Medici, and Bartolomeo Cristofori—" he pauses and looks at Bart, who turns bright red. "—we welcome you to The Creation of Music. Today, you will hear a new instrument, the first of its kind in all of history." Andy's voice carries itself to each person's ears with clarity, captivating everyone.

"At first glance, one might assume this instrument is the same as a harpsichord. I assure you it is not. What you are about to hear is a two-decade-long vision of mine and a seventeen-year project for Bartolomeo, the genius behind, and inventor of, the piano. I have multiple tunes composed specifically for the piano, crafted to show all of its unique features, but the first tune I'll play..." turning from the audience, Andy walks back to the piano and sits down, continuing to speak... "is one I wrote for its creator." Andy turns and looks again at Bart, his smile even brighter than before, and Bart again feels himself blushing. He can barely contain his thrill over Andy's showmanship, his pitch-perfect presentation. It is such a fitting tribute, more than he ever dreamed it could be.

Andy's wife, Marsha, leans over to Adele and Bart. "This one is for Cuori."

Bart reaches for Adele's hand and squeezes it, preparing to cry in front of a thousand people.

Andy begins to play, so quietly in the treble clef at first that Bart thinks the tune is a lullaby, but then he gradually adds harmony in the bass clef, making the music more dynamic but still soft. He strikes the keys with precision, his eyes closed in concentration.

Bart can feel the gentle vibrations from the strings of the piano within his chest. He thinks of Cuori, and memories he had forgotten come to life in his mind. The conversations they had when she was a small but brilliant child. And the way he used to pick her up in his arms and twirl her in the air. He closes his eyes now, too, but it doesn't stop his tears.

Adele caresses his forearm with her hand, which helps him relax and keeps him from falling apart. He knows she is seeing and hearing their daughter's laugh and smile as clearly as he is.

Andy's fingers begin traveling toward the middle of the keyboard, where they gently kiss a single note. Just when it seems the tune might be finished, he starts again. This time, he plays more quickly in the bass clef with aggrandizing loudness, cascading into a heart-pounding melody.

The power of the music from the piano's intense vibrations shakes the room. Bart notices beads of sweat appear on Andy's forehead. Looking over the audience, he sees they are swept away in the bliss of smooth chords broken up in eighth notes. Now, as Andy begins playing an ethereal melody in the treble clef, the audience becomes mesmerized. Bart's focus returns to Andy's hands, pounding out an angelic voice, and he feels it tear at the hearts of everyone in the auditorium.

For himself, he feels as if he is floating as memory upon memory of his daughter flood his mind. He cries not out of sadness but from gratitude. "Thank you," he whispers to God. "She was perfect."

Adele rests her head on his shoulder now, and he senses she is overwhelmed with emotion, too. This must be what heaven sounds like, he thinks.

As the piece continues, the crescendo and decrescendo create a dynamic sound that Bart knows has never been heard from any instrument before. It's as if a choir of a thousand voices lives inside the body of the piano. Andy's hands slow, his touch softens, and he finishes the tune the same way it began, and the only way Bart can describe it is as a masterful lullaby.

In the ensuing moments following the last fading note, the room is utterly silent. Not even a breath can be heard. But when the audience realizes the composition is over, like a tsunami wave, every person rises to their feet, shouting and clapping. Bart, Adele, and the whole group sitting on the stage follow suit. Andy stands, too, bowing to the crowd, then he bows to Bart and Adele.

Stepping back to the piano, he sits down, but he is unable to resume play for the next piece given the continuing and thunderous applause from the crowd. Bart hears the shriek of whistling. Glancing at Andy, he sees the musician laughing. It's hard for him to accept such praise, Bart thinks, and he shares the feeling. He, himself, is overwhelmed.

Finally, placing his hand over his heart, Andy rises and facing the audience he mouths, "Thank you." A moment later, he approaches Bart, and grasping his shoulder, he pulls him to the center of the stage.

The nervousness Bart had earlier is gone, eclipsed by a sense of triumph. Along with Andy, he bows before the roaring throng of admirers and the celebratory show of appreciation grows even louder. As if borne on the wave of adulation, Bart jogs back to Adele and tugs her out to the stage's center, gesturing with his hands, giving her the credit for the piano.

"What are you doing?" Adele asks, peering at him in confusion.

He barely hears her over the crowd. "You should probably bow," he tells her.

"But why?"

He glances down at her. "I couldn't have done it without you."

Her face softens, becoming full of humility, and turning her gaze to the crowd, she does as Bart instructed. His heart swells as she takes a bow, too. He, Adele, and Andy stand together, smiling, and Bart wonders if his wife's face and his friend's face hurt from the stretch the way his does.

Andy, the dreamer. Bart, the inventor. Adele, the reason. The notion runs through Bart's mind.

"This changes everything." Andy addresses Bart, and he nods, feeling the truth of Andy's words in his bones.

[Listen to 'The Creation of Music']

CHAPTER
Thirty-seven

Bart

*T*he table is laden with food and surrounded by people. Bart retrieved extra chairs so that everyone could fit inside the Cristofori's dining room. Molly and Sheila have hardly stopped talking. Their similar personalities give them endless things to discuss, Bart thinks. Anna and Adele have spent the entire evening catching up. By the persistent smiles on both their faces, it is evident they missed each other equally as much. Frank and his wife sit at one end of the table, and Andy and his wife the other, with everyone else in the middle. Bart included.

Although The Creation of Music ended hours ago, the energy from the event still courses through Bart's veins. What happened today was far greater than he could have possibly imagined. He knew the piano's strength and powerful emotional capabilities but was unprepared for the splendor of Andy's compositions or the crowd's resounding and enthusiastic response. He still can't believe the standing ovation for the first tune lasted so long!

Bart exchanges a grin with Marco, who serves himself and everyone else their food. When he sets the final plate of pasta down on the table, Dario fills each wine glass, describing its history and flavors as he pours. Bart holds Adele's hand, her presence an overwhelming comfort.

"Ready to begin our meal?" Marco asks once Dario sits down.

There is a murmured, collective, "Yes."

But before anyone can begin eating, Andy pushes his chair back and, standing, he lifts his wine glass and says, "I want to make a toast."

There is the clatter of cutlery being set aside, and Bart, like the other guests, focuses on Andy.

He begins by clearing his throat. "Today, history was made. People from all across Italy came to Florence to witness the debut of a new instrument we have named the piano. I have been around music my whole life, and I'm old, but I have never seen an audience so moved." He pauses and looks around at those assembled. "Seventeen years ago," he continues, "I approached Bart. I had a dream for an instrument that could play in a lyrical fashion and both piano and forte, one that would respond to the emotions of the musician in real time. Today, I experienced that dream come alive in dramatic proportions."

Those at the table, including Bart, exchange smiles and nod in agreement with Andy.

He says, "When I was playing today, I had visions of the future where musicians will have had the piano their whole lives, and the music they create will last throughout their lifetime and centuries after. I could see it being the most popular instrument, picked by the most talented musicians worldwide because of its distinct ability to connect to its composer. I see it in households where the deepest secrets and most complex emotions are brought to the surface through melody and harmony. I see how music now has the ability to raise up hope in a chaotic world. We all witnessed that."

Grunts of agreement fill the dining room.

"The piano has changed music forever and, subsequently, the world. This is due entirely to one incredible man, whom I am immensely blessed to have been able to work with and privileged to call my friend, Bart."

When Andy finds his gaze, Bart feels the eyes of all those assembled on him, too, and the heat he felt prior to Andy's performance again crawls over his face. Somehow, the attention of those he knows is just as intimidating as a thousand strangers.

"Bart, nobody will ever know the discipline, the pain, or the grit required of you to invent the piano except you and the people in this room, but the world will be eternally grateful for you and what you have accomplished. To Bart! The man who invented the piano and all that comes next!" Andy shouts, and everyone raises their glass.

Bart jumps to his feet now too. "To Andy!" he cries. "The man who found a way to make his dream come true!"

The two exchange a grin, sharing their mutual pride and admiration. A chorus of huzzahs and the crystalline sound of glasses being clinked fills the air. Andy and Bart are still standing when Adele rises from her chair beside him. Light from the evening sun radiates around her, and to Bart she is an elegant vision clothed in gold. To him she looks like a queen.

She raises her glass and says, "To the moment when a dreamer and an inventor changed the world!"

The End.

Acknowledgements

This novel would not have been possible without numerous friends and family supporting me along the way. The first person I want to thank is my dad, James Bell. He wouldn't let me quit piano lessons as a child, even though I thought they were boring. What I felt at the time was his being mean was really him not letting me settle for what is easy but pushing through what is hard to earn a gift and ability that can never be taken away. Because of piano lessons, I am able to write and play music, but it is also what inspired my interest in the piano. Thank you, Dad. This brings me to the second person I want to thank, Sheri Noble, my piano teacher. Sheri taught me how to play the piano from when I was nine to when I was seventeen. Her kind and gentle nature is exactly what I needed as a student to learn.

I want to thank Barbara Sissel, my editor. She tore the storyline apart and revealed all its weaknesses, allowing me to marry it back together, which crafted the beautiful story you hold in your hands that I can be so proud of. Thank you, Barbara, for your honesty and creativity. I also want to thank Matt and Jennifer Knapp. These two generously agreed to beta-read The Creation of Music before it had any other editing work besides mine. They both thoroughly enjoyed it and gave me incredibly valuable and honest feedback. My sister-in-law, DaVay Rutledge, graciously agreed to proofread the novel the final time before it was formatted for printing. Thank you, DaVay, for your help in making The Creation of Music the best it can be.

I am deeply grateful to Edgel Barrientos for his exceptional work in designing the cover for The Creation of Music and formatting the interior so beautifully. I also want to extend my heartfelt thanks to all of my friends and family for their unwavering support and love. I could not have written a story so focused on the power of relationships without their presence in my life.

Lastly, I want to credit my mother, Heather Bell, with inspiring me to be an author. She is in heaven now, but I want to honor her as though she were still here. Mom, because of you, I am not afraid to try. I am not afraid of failure. I watched your strength and grit carry you through to your last day, and in the end, you won. You are where we all long to be. I know I can do anything, no matter how badly it hurts or how long it takes, because you showed me it's possible. The reward may not be on earth, but it is heaven itself. It is the hope we have in Jesus that is my reward. So, I pursue my dreams, even into the unknown, because you paved the way. I love you. Forever.

About the Author

BRITIAN BELL is an artist, author, and visionary who is passionate about loving people, songwriting, storytelling, and inspiring a better world.

He was born in the heart of the Ozarks in Missouri and has lived there his whole life. He grew up on a farm, surrounded by family and friends. His families farm had many acres of land to explore, which helped him craft and expand his imagination. Family and faith were and still are enormous influences in his life, developing a love for people inside him that grows more each day. His love for writing began at the age of twenty, and published his first novel, *A World Full of Beautiful People*, at the age of twenty-two.

9 798218 423650